Sacred Glasgow and the Clyde Valley

To Dad

Happy Birthday 2016
Love
Richard.

✗ HOMEWORK - Study Church No. 49.

SACRED PLACES SERIES

Sacred Glasgow and the Clyde Valley

SCOTLAND'S CHURCHES SCHEME

SAINT ANDREW PRESS
Edinburgh

First published in 2010 by
SAINT ANDREW PRESS
121 George Street
Edinburgh EH2 4YN

ISBN 978 0 7152 0946 2

British Library Cataloguing in Publication Data
A catalogue record for this book is available from the British Library.

Typeset in Enigma by Waverley Typesetters, Warham, Norfolk
Manufactured in Great Britain by Bell & Bain Ltd, Glasgow

BUCKINGHAM PALACE

As Patron of Scotland's Churches Scheme, I warmly welcome this publication as part of the *Sacred Places* series of books being produced by the Scheme.

The story of the heritage and culture of Scotland would be lacking significantly without a strong focus on its churches and sacred sites. I am sure that this guidebook will be a source of information and enjoyment both to the people of Scotland and to our visitors.

Anne

Scotland's Churches Scheme

www.sacredscotland.org.uk

Scotland's Churches Scheme is an ecumenical charitable trust, providing an opportunity to access the nation's living heritage of faith by assisting the 'living' churches in membership to:

- Promote spiritual understanding by enabling the public to appreciate all buildings designed for worship and active as living churches
- Work together with others to make the Church the focus of the community
- Open their doors with a welcoming presence
- Tell the story of the building (however old or new), its purpose and heritage (artistic, architectural and historical)
- Provide information for visitors, young and old

The Scheme has grown rapidly since its inception in 1994, and there are now more than 1,200 churches in membership. These churches are spread across Scotland and across the denominations.

The *Sacred Scotland* theme promoted by Scotland's Churches Scheme focuses on the wish of both visitors and local communities to be able to access our wonderful range of church buildings in a meaningful way, whether the visit be occasioned by spiritual or heritage motivation or both. The Scheme can advise and assist member churches on visitor welcome, and, with its range of 'how-to' brochures, provide information on research, presentation, security and other live issues. The Scheme, with its network of local representatives, encourages the opening of doors and the care of tourists and locals alike, and offers specific services such as the provision of grants for organ-playing.

Sacred Scotland (www.sacredscotland.org.uk), the website of Scotland's Churches Scheme, opens the door to Scotland's story by exploring living traditions of faith in city, town, village and island across the country.

The site is a portal to access information on Scotland's churches of all denominations and is a starting point for your special journeys.

We are delighted to be working with Saint Andrew Press in the publication of this series of regional guides to Scotland's churches. In 2009, the first three volumes were published – *Sacred South-West Scotland*; *Sacred Fife and the Forth Valley*; and *Sacred Edinburgh and Midlothian*. This volume, *Sacred Glasgow and the Clyde Valley*, is one of three being published in 2010 (the others are *Sacred North-East Scotland* and *Sacred Borders and East Lothian*), to be followed by a further three books in 2011, when the whole country will have been covered. We are grateful to the authors of the introductory articles, Professor John Hume, one of our Trustees, and Cath Doherty, for their expert contributions to our understanding of sacred places.

The growth of 'spiritual tourism' worldwide is reflected in the million-plus people who visit Scotland's religious sites annually. We hope that the information in this book will be useful in bringing alive the heritage as well as the ministry of welcome which our churches offer. In the words of our former President, Lady Marion Fraser: 'we all owe a deep debt of gratitude to the many people of vision who work hard and imaginatively to create a lasting and peaceful atmosphere which you will carry away with you as a special memory when you leave'.

DR BRIAN FRASER
Director
Scotland's Churches Scheme
Dunedin
Holehouse Road
Eaglesham
Glasgow
G76 0JF

Invitation to Pilgrimage

Glasgow and the Clyde Valley

The Footprints of History

The vast spread of the city of Glasgow dominates the west of Scotland, reaching out to encompass East Renfrewshire and East Dunbartonshire. To the south, and running east of the city, are neighbouring North and South Lanarkshire. This city and its environs are rich in the history of sacred places which hold echoes of majesty and grandeur, memories of ancient saints and the patronage of kings. Through the ages, they have borne the marks of both conflict and reconciliation. They are testament to belief, to spiritual strength. All of them bear the footprints of history.

The Path of Ancient Saints

North of Glasgow's High Street stands the Cathedral Church of St Mungo. Here, in the fifth century, St Ninian consecrated ground for burial. St Mungo built a small wooden church here, instituting the site as a place of worship. In his travels from Whithorn, St Ninian may also have come to Govan, at that time a small farming village on the banks of the Clyde, consecrating ground for burial on the site of what is now Govan Old Parish Church. Govan later became the spiritual centre of the ancient kingdom of Strathclyde, a place where nobility sought the right to burial.

In Stonehouse, South Lanarkshire, St Ninian is said to have scattered earth brought from Whithorn on an escarpment above the River Avon, choosing it as a place where the Church of St Ninian was to be built. Thus, he left his footprints in the west, as did St Mungo in the sixth century and beyond. Today, the tomb of Glasgow's patron saint lies in the lower reaches of Glasgow Cathedral. His grave is thought to lie nearby.

St Conval, son of an Irish prince and spiritual disciple of Mungo, is associated with the area now known as East Renfrewshire. Here, in the sixth century, he formed religious settlements in Eastwood and Barrhead. St Mirin is similarly associated with Paisley. St Machan, trained in Ireland, devoted his life to his mission in the Clyde Valley, his religious centre at Dalserf once known as Machanshire. St Serf, usually associated with Culross on the River Forth, also worked to spread Christianity in the Clyde Valley.

Monastic Foundations

A very early monastic foundation existed in Govan. It was dedicated to St Constantine, a Cornish saint. Assisted by the patronage of successive kings and nobles, the Cluniacs came to Paisley and the Augustinians to Blantyre, and hospitals were established by monks in places such as Crookston, Polmadie and Torrance. An ancient charter given by William the Lion towards the end of the twelfth century records the gifting of lands to be known as Monklands to the Bishopric of Glasgow; this, the king wrote, 'for the safety of my soul'. There were many such gifts of land between the twelfth and fifteenth centuries; another charter recorded in the reign of Robert II outlined the endowment of land near Motherwell to Paisley Abbey. During this period of monastic growth, the significance of the Bishopric of Glasgow grew. On the site of what is now the Cathedral, a stone church was built and consecrated in the presence of David I in 1136. Destroyed by fire, it was replaced in 1197.

Thereafter came a rich period in which the Bishopric of Glasgow endowed many places of worship across the west. As they did, monastic foundations served the needs of the people not only in matters spiritual but also in reclamation and cultivation of land, and care of the sick and the poor. Cistercians came from the valley of the Esk, building a road which ran through Airdrie and trading their wagons of lead ore through the monastic settlement in Rutherglen.

The all-embracing nature of the Bishopric of Glasgow might best be illustrated by the issuing of a Papal Bull by Pope Sixtus IV in 1476, which agreed to the endowing of St Catherine's Chapel at Shotts, some eight miles distant from the Church of St Mary in Bothwell. Shotts was described as 'a cold and infertile mountain region, where many of the inhabitants die without receiving the church sacraments'.

In 1490, the Dean of Glasgow Cathedral was also secretary to King James IV, and thus the close connections between Church and State at this time can be illustrated.

A Growing City

With the emergence of the Reformation in the sixteenth century, the monastic foundations came to an end and the religious landscape changed. Glasgow Cathedral itself was protected from damage in the turbulence of this period by the intervention of the trades of Glasgow, who united in defence of their historic building. Today it still stands in Gothic splendour, a treasure store of 1,500 years of history. It remains a place of worship.

The nineteenth century brought both growth and change to the west. An industrial revolution saw the arrival of Highland workers, followed by Irish immigrants who came to the textile mills and shipyards. For Catholics, the restoration of the hierarchy meant freedom to practise their religion. New churches were built to serve the needs of a rapidly growing population of Catholics in Glasgow. St Andrew's Cathedral was completed in 1817. St Mary's Calton was completed in 1842 and welcomed congregations said to number over 1,000. It is particularly associated with the Irish immigrants who fled famine in the mid-nineteenth century. Govan Old Parish Church drew many Highland, Gaelic-speaking members to their congregation, which was later to be associated with the Iona Community.

As Glasgow grew to become known as the Second City of the Empire, so its places of worship grew, nurturing the communities that sprang up around them. In all of them is a sense of continuity and, somehow, a reflection of the generosity of spirit found in the west. Glasgow Cathedral and Paisley Abbey, painstakingly and gloriously restored to the finest detail, are places of worship which honour history. The ancient stones of Govan, the copestone of St Mary's Well at Motherwell, the stones of antiquity at Cambusnethan, Dalserf, Bothwell, the sites of holy wells, the place names telling of the past ... all are examples of the unbroken thread of history that links sacred places, places of worship.

These sacred places reflect the lives of the people who gathered there for prayer and praise: the small Pugin church in a Lanarkshire village, built by miners who shared the fruits of their labours; the Church of St Simon in Partick which welcomed Polish troops during the Second World War and once again welcomes the stranger with Masses for Polish immigrants; Govan Old Parish Church, which became the centre of a complete community, preserving the culture of the people who came there in the nineteenth century.

Glasgow, a city of spires, is also a cosmopolitan city; this is reflected in the architecture of a significant number of its places of worship. The Milton Free Church in St Vincent Street is an imposing building of classical style, with Egyptian, Indian and Assyrian influences, and is known as the masterpiece of its architect, Alexander 'Greek' Thomson. In Buchanan Street, St George's Tron Parish Church has a distinctive outline, its Baroque-styled tower topped by a ribbed dome and obelisk. Garnethill Synagogue, the first purpose-built synagogue in Scotland, completed in 1879, favours a striking Romanesque-cum-Byzantine style of architecture. St Aloysius, Rose Street, was built to a Renaissance design at the beginning of the twentieth century, its architect Belgian, its finely decorated marble interior completed by an Austrian architect.

Glasgow and the Clyde Valley is a region of warmth, of contrasts, of welcome. The city itself is known for its outreach to others, so it is fitting that many of its places of worship reflect these marks of identity. Renfield St Stephen's Church and Centre in Bath Street provides an example of this with its extension of offices, halls and restaurant giving an opportunity of outreach to the wider community. In Bath Street also, the Adelaide Place Baptist Church has replaced decay with renewal and expansion of the building, again providing for the needs of the extended community.

The city and surrounding region are rich in places of worship which mirror their history, their diversity, their eagerness to meet the future. And, in their many sacred places, the very essence of that worship lives and grows day by day.

CATH DOHERTY
Scottish Catholic Observer

Introduction

Sacred Glasgow and the Clyde Valley

Before about AD 1100, Dumbarton, further west, and then Govan (now within the Glasgow boundary) appear to have been the major centres of civil and religious power in the Clyde valley, with Rutherglen latterly a rival trading centre. The sculptured stones in Govan Old Parish Church (**63**), dating from the ninth and tenth centuries AD, testify to the place's significance at that time. Glasgow's rise to become the most important trading, religious and educational centre in west central Scotland seems to have begun in the twelfth century, but it was only in the later eighteenth century that its population began to grow significantly. By the late nineteenth century, Glasgow could justifiably claim to be the 'Second City of the Empire'. Much of the city's growth was due to its increasingly complex role as a regional capital, supplying a wide range of services, including education at all levels. By 1914, Glasgow was one of the most advanced cities in the world. A distinctive feature of the city was the density of its population. Many of its inhabitants lived in tenements, until the early twentieth century often without decent sanitation. However, the compactness of the built-up area created a manageable city. Not until the 1920s did serious suburban sprawl develop, though good railway and steamer services led to the development of outer suburban areas in the country and on the Firth of Clyde. Some are now in East Renfrewshire and East Dunbartonshire, and are hence included in this volume.

From the early nineteenth century, migrants from other parts of Scotland, from Ireland and, to a lesser extent, from England, Italy and Central Europe poured into the city. Many were Roman Catholic, and a feature of the city is the number of churches built to accommodate them. In the later nineteenth century, many European Jews moved to Glasgow, and the first synagogue in Scotland was constructed in Garnethill in 1879; later, many Jews moved into East Renfrewshire.

Glasgow's growth had a significant impact on its hinterland. The administrative reorganisation of Scotland in the eleventh and twelfth centuries divided the country into parishes, grouped into dioceses, and planted towns in strategic places as trading centres. Glasgow was one; so too were Rutherglen, Hamilton and Lanark, all in their day comparable to Glasgow. Rutherglen was, for a time, the head of navigation on the Clyde; Hamilton became the

Fig. 1. The former St Bride's Collegiate Church, Douglas, South Lanarkshire

seat of the area's premier landowning family, the Hamiltons; Lanark was the market town for the upper Clyde Valley and gave its name to the county. It was a large county, and for administration was divided into three 'wards': the Upper Ward was centred on Lanark, the Middle on Hamilton, and the Lower on Glasgow. By the late eighteenth century, new burghs had been founded at Airdrie in the east and Douglas (Fig. 1) in the south-west. Other centres of populations were developing, including Bothwell, Cambuslang, Cambusnethan, East Kilbride and Strathaven.

The area was transformed from the mid-eighteenth century by industrialisation linked to foreign trade. Early industries included hand-spinning and weaving of linen. The introduction of mechanical cotton-spinning in the late eighteenth century greatly magnified the scale of production. Water-powered spinning mills were established at New Lanark, Blantyre, Neilston and Barrhead, and smaller ones elsewhere. The availability of unprecedented quantities of yarn led to the expansion of handloom weaving, transforming Airdrie, Kilsyth, Larkhall, Strathaven and some of Glasgow's suburbs. From the 1790s, steam power was applied to cotton-spinning, especially in Glasgow, and within a few years steam was also being used to power weaving factories, especially in Glasgow and Airdrie. Bleaching and calico-printing also flourished for a time, for instance in Pollokshaws and Maryhill. More radically transforming, however, was exploitation from the later eighteenth century of the extensive seams of coal and ironstone of the lower Clyde basin, aided by the construction of canals and railways. This created four major new settlements – Coatbridge,

Motherwell, Shotts and Wishaw – as well as a number of smaller ones and many short-lived mining villages. Glasgow became the administrative centre for both the textile and mineral-based industries of the area. As a result, the middle-class populations of most of the industrial communities remained relatively small. As the middle classes were, for the Protestant denominations, their leading supporters, this affected the scale and character of church-building outside the city.

The last major shifts in population in the area came after the First World War. The decline of iron-smelting and associated mining resulted in mass emigration. The rehousing of the remaining population began in the early 1920s and gained momentum after the Second World War. Overcrowding in central Glasgow was tackled after the war by building large peripheral housing estates and by creating the 'New Towns' of East Kilbride and Cumbernauld. In the 1960s and 1970s, many of the older tenemented areas of Glasgow were demolished and rebuilt.

These transformations since the 1780s have dominated church-building, rebuilding and disuse to the extent that it is impossible to understand the church history of the area without some background historical understanding. Thus there are relatively few churches dating from before the mid-eighteenth century in whole or in part; then a group dating from the period of agricultural improvement in the eighteenth and early nineteenth centuries (Fig. 2). There are some fine, large churches associated with the expansion of the textile, coal and iron industries (and of Glasgow) in the first half of the nineteenth century, and then a great number of churches linked to urban and suburban expansion between 1850 and 1914. The building of new churches during the last period was, as elsewhere in Scotland, strongly influenced by denominational complexity,

Fig. 2. The former St Andrew's Church of Scotland, St Andrew's Square, Glasgow

Fig. 3. St Anthony's Roman Catholic Church,
Govan Road, Glasgow

variety and competition. The continuing effects of the eighteenth-century secessions, the creation of the Free Church in 1843 and of the United Presbyterian Church in 1847, Roman Catholic immigration (Fig. 3), and the resurgence of the Scottish Episcopal Church in the later nineteenth century all had an impact.

As elsewhere in Scotland, few churches were built between 1914 and 1945; but, between the 1940s and the 1970s, major housing developments resulted in the construction of large numbers of churches, principally by the Church of Scotland and the Roman Catholic Church. The period since the 1960s has also been characterised by a drastic reduction in the number of churches, particularly Church of Scotland buildings, in urban areas, especially in Glasgow – a process which continues and has been extended into the industrial areas.

The rest of this Introduction is arranged geographically, roughly by local-authority area. After Glasgow come North and South Lanarkshire, taken together. North Lanarkshire includes parts of the former Dunbartonshire and Stirlingshire. East Dunbartonshire follows, and finally East Renfrewshire is discussed. Because of the number of churches in the area, individual buildings are only mentioned selectively, and the emphasis is on surviving buildings.

The City of Glasgow

The oldest church building in the city is the cathedral, first built in the twelfth century, but replaced from the thirteenth century by the present building (1, Fig. 4). It survived the Reformation with its roof intact and was divided into three churches for Reformed worship. The interior was reunited and restored in the mid-nineteenth century. In the late sixteenth century, a new church was built on the Trongate, whose tower and spire survive as the Tron Steeple. During the late seventeenth century, another church was built to serve the growing western areas of the city. Its successor, the 'Ramshorn Church' (1824–6; now a theatre, Fig. 5), survives (see below).

Fig. 4. Glasgow Cathedral

Further expansion led to the building of two important new churches in the mid-eighteenth century. St Andrew's Parish Church (completed 1756; now a concert hall) was built for the Church of Scotland – the largest and finest Scottish church built since the Reformation. St Andrew-by-the-Green, close by (now offices), was constructed for the Scottish Episcopal Church. In about 1790, the body of the Tron Church was destroyed by fire, then rebuilt (1794; now a theatre). In 1807, St George's Church (**6**; now St George's Tron) was built on Buchanan Street to serve western expansion. Out in the country, Carmunnock Parish Church (**43**) was built in 1767. It is now within the city boundary. Also outside the built-up area, Govan's medieval church was replaced by a simple Gothic Revival building (1820; later replaced), and so too was Cathcart's, the tower of which (1831) survives.

Glasgow's growth brought religious diversity. The eighteenth-century secessions flourished, and many other denominations developed. The Roman Catholics completed what is now St Andrew's Cathedral (**2**) in 1816, their first church in Glasgow since the Reformation, and a landmark early Gothic Revival building. Their second church in the city, St Mary's, Calton (1842), is classical though not strictly so. The reunion of many of the Secession churches in 1820 as the United Secession Church was followed by the building of several new churches, none of which now survives. One of the last new churches

Fig. 5. The doorway of the former St David's Ramshorn Church of Scotland, Ingram Street, Glasgow

Fig. 6. Pollokshaws Parish Church, Shawbridge Street, Glasgow

built before the 1840s was the Greek Revival St Jude's Scottish Episcopal Church, West George Street (1838-9; now part of a hotel).

The first of the revolutionary events of the 1840s was the creation of the Free Church by the Disruption in the Church of Scotland in 1843. The second was the union in 1847 of the United Secession Church and the Relief Church (another eighteenth-century secession) to form the United Presbyterian Church. Other secession churches combined to form the Original Secession Church, one of whose congregations built in 1843 what is now Pollokshaws Parish Church (Fig. 6). In an increasingly wealthy and populous community, the two new denominations competed vigorously with each other, and with the Church of Scotland, for the rest of the nineteenth century. This competition resulted in the creation of many buildings of exceptional architectural quality, some internationally important. The least altered early Free church in the city is the former St Andrew's Free, North Hanover Street (1844; now a furniture store). Of three large churches built in the city centre in the 1840s, none now exists. The earliest, St John's Free in George Street (1845), was the first large steepled Gothic Revival church in the city. The oldest surviving city-centre church in use is Renfield St Stephen's (7, 1852, originally Independent), another representative of that type. Its adjacent church centre was largely funded by the sale in the 1960s of the massive Renfield Street United Presbyterian Church (1848).

In the mid-1850s, the rate of church-building began to increase due to the expansion of middle-class suburbs to the east, west and south of the old city centre. In the east, Sydney Place, Duke Street (1857-8; now offices, Fig. 7), and, in the south, Caledonia Road (1856-7; now ruined) were built for the United Presbyterians, who also

Fig. 7. The former Sydney Place United Presbyterian Church, Duke Street, Glasgow

constructed St Vincent Street (**9**, 1859) and John Street (1859–60; now offices and restaurant) nearer the city centre. All of these were classical. The quality of design of these buildings was exceptional, reflecting the wealth and taste of Glasgow's citizens. During the same period, the Established Church built Sandyford Henderson Memorial (**16**, 1855) and Park (1856–8; tower only survives) churches, and the Roman Catholics what is now St Simon's, Partick (**22**, 1858). These are all Gothic Revival.

Denominational rivalry gained momentum in the 1860s and 1870s as the expansion of the city continued. By that time, the steepled Gothic Revival had become almost universally fashionable. Major surviving churches of this type built in the 1860s include Kelvinside (1862, Free; now a leisure complex), Lansdowne (**20**, 1863, United Presbyterian), Eastwood (**48**, 1863, Church of Scotland), Claremont Congregational (1864; now a concert hall), Townhead (1865–6, Church of Scotland; steeple only survives), Dowanhill (1865–6, United Presbyterian; now a theatre) and Ibrox United Presbyterian (1867–8; now a climbing centre). From the 1870s, there are the former Queen's Park High (1873, Church of Scotland; now flats), St Mary's Scottish Episcopal Cathedral (**12**, 1871–4, steeple added 1893), the former Dennistoun Central (1873–4, Free), the former Woodlands United Presbyterian Church, now St Jude's Free Presbyterian Church (1874–5), Queen's Park (**53**, 1873–5, Free), Camphill Queen's Park, now Queen's Park Baptist Church (**52**, 1875–8, United Presbyterian, spire completed 1883), and Pollokshields (**57**, 1877–8, Church of Scotland).

Not all Gothic churches of the period had steeples. Dennistoun Parish (1869–70, United Presbyterian) has a tower, and some churches had neither tower nor steeple. Of these, St Luke's Greek Orthodox Cathedral (**13**), formerly Belhaven United Presbyterian Church (1877), is notably distinguished, with its frontage modelled on Dunblane Cathedral. Simpler Gothic churches of the period include St Ninian's Scottish Episcopal Church, Pollokshields (**56**, 1872–7) and Govanhill (1878–80, United Presbyterian, Fig. 8).

Fig. 8. Govanhill Parish Church, Daisy Street, Glasgow

Fig. 9. The former Belhaven Westbourne
(ex-Westbourne Free) Church,
Westbourne Gardens, Glasgow

The most remarkable surviving church of the mid-Victorian period is probably Kelvinside Hillhead (**21**, 1876, Church of Scotland), with a semi-circular east end and an interior unobstructed by columns. Adelaide Place Baptist Church (1877; now Adelaide's, **10**), Glasgow Evangelical Church (1876–80, originally Cathedral Square United Presbyterian) and Finnieston Free (1878–80; now flats) embody classical detailing in more free-form designs. Garnethill Synagogue (**11**, 1879), Glasgow's first, St Anthony's Roman Catholic Church, Govan (1877–9, Fig. 3) and the former Blackfriars Parish Church, Dennistoun (1878; now flats) are all in variants of the Romanesque.

In the 1880s, there were two important trends in church design in Glasgow: a renewal of interest in the Greek Revival, and a more original approach to the Gothic Revival. The free approach to classicism developed in the later 1870s continued in Westbourne Free (1880–1; now an evangelical church, Fig. 9) with two tiers of columns, and in Nithsdale United Presbyterian Church, Pollokshields (1888; now a care home) with a baroque steeple. Hillhead Baptist (1883) is a smaller version of Adelaide's. The most impressive classical churches of the period are Wellington (**18**, 1884) and St George's in the Fields (1885–6; now flats, Fig. 10), both for the United Presbyterians. The great Gothic Revival churches of the 1880s were all built for the Church of Scotland, and all embodied the Ecclesiological Movement's return to medieval patterns of church layout. Hyndland (**27**, 1887) was the first, followed by Govan Old (**63**, 1888) and

Fig. 10. The former St George's in the Fields
Parish Church, Woodside, Glasgow

Barony (1886–9; now a graduation hall). Shawlands Old (1888–9; now an evangelical church) and Cardonald (**61**, 1889) are smaller examples of this trend. Govan Old and Hyndland were intended to have spires, but these were not completed.

During the 1890s, there was a significant change in emphasis in church-building. On the one hand, construction began of a series of large churches for the Roman Catholics, and on the other the Free and United Presbyterian churches began programmes of church extension in areas of new housing. Most of the Roman Catholic churches, as in surrounding areas (see below), were designed by the London architects Pugin & Pugin and have a strong family resemblance. Most of these have survived. The oldest in the city is St Bridget's, Baillieston (**41**, 1893), and it was followed by St Agnes's, Lambhill (1893–4) and St Patrick's, Anderston (**14**, 1898). The last large nineteenth-century Presbyterian Gothic Revival church to be built was Pollokshields Trinity United Presbyterian (1890–1; demolished), and the last big classical church was Langside Hill United Presbyterian (1894–6; now a restaurant, Fig. 11). Most other churches built in the 1890s were fairly modest in scale and conventionally Gothic. A notable exception was Queen's Cross, Garscube Road (1896–9, Free), Charles Rennie Mackintosh's only church, and an Art Nouveau building of exceptional quality, now a monument to its designer. The other, much less well known, is the first church of St Andrew's East, Alexandra Parade (1899, Free), designed by James Salmon the younger and J. Gaff Gillespie as a hall prior to the construction of the church. It has recently reverted to being the place of worship. It is also Art Nouveau, but of a very different, more modest and human kind.

The Free Church was particularly active in church extension towards the end of the 1890s – but, before some of these churches could be completed, that denomination united with the United Presbyterians in 1900 to form the United Free Church. Sherbrooke St Gilbert's (**58**), Kelvin Stevenson Memorial, Govan Linthouse (**65**, now Linthouse St Kenneth's) and Victoria Tollcross, completed by the new Church in 1900–2, were all

Fig. 11. The former Langside Hill Church of Scotland, Langside Road, Glasgow

Fig. 12. Shettleston New Parish Church (formerly Eastbank), Glasgow

initially planned by the Free Church. Kelvin Stevenson Memorial was designed as a training church for Free (United Free) ministers, and, with its crown steeple, is more elaborate than most. The new Church continued the programme of church extension from then until the First World War. During that period, more than a dozen United Free churches were built. Most of them have a family resemblance, in English Perpendicular style, built of red or cream sandstone, and with comfortable galleried interiors. Broomhill (**26**, 1902) and the Macgregor Memorial, Govan (1902–4; demolished) had towers, the former with a tiled spire; and New Cathcart (1907–8; now flats) has a small spire. The others include Newlands South (1901–3), Ruchill (1905), Temple Anniesland (**30**, 1905), Scotstoun East (1904–6), Battlefield East (**47**, 1912) and South Shawlands (**50**, 1913). The most interesting architecturally of these United Free churches are Eastbank, Shettleston (1901–4, Fig. 12) and St Andrew's East (1903–4; now flats, Fig. 13). Eastbank is externally a fairly typical United Free church, with a red-tiled spire. Internally, however, it has a fine, vigorous Arts and Crafts worship space. The hall of St Andrew's East has been mentioned above; the church has a dramatically tall arched frontage to Alexandra Parade, which eclipses the hall. Its interior was very plain.

The other major denominations were less prolific church-builders in the years before the First World War. Church of Scotland buildings included St Margaret's Tollcross (1901), a small but beautifully detailed Arts and Crafts church, Shettleston Old (**38**, 1903), a very handsome but unadventurous

Fig. 13. St Andrew's East Parish Church, Glasgow

Gothic building, the grandiose steepled St Columba's Gaelic Church, St Vincent Street (1902–4) and the modest, towered Jordanhill (**31**, 1905). The last Church of Scotland buildings constructed in this period were Balshagray (1907–12) and Merrylea (1912–15). The former is conventionally Gothic, and the latter is a fine example of the scholarly Romanesque Revival work of Peter Macgregor Chalmers. So, too, is the Scottish Episcopal church of St Margaret's, Newlands (**49**), construction of which started in 1910. The other Episcopal churches of the period are All Saints, Jordanhill (1904) and St Bride's, Hyndland (**25**, 1904 and later). For the Roman Catholic Church, Pugin & Pugin designed St Peter's, Partick (**23**, 1903), St Alphonsus, Calton (**3**, 1905) and Holy Cross, Crosshill (**54**, 1911); the first two are Gothic, the third Romanesque. More adventurously, the Belgian C. J. Menart produced Italianate designs for the Sacred Heart, Bridgeton (1900–10) and St Aloysius, Garnethill (**5**, 1908–10). Both incorporate early reinforced concrete in their construction. St Aloysius has a notable interior, with extensive mural decoration. Several Congregational churches date from this time. The most interesting is Broomhill Trinity (1900–8; now apartments), the only example of the 'low-line' churches designed by Sir J. J. Burnet and built from the early 1890s. This was Burnet's own church.

A few churches begun before 1914 were completed during the First World War, but that war brought an effective end to church-building. The early interwar years were difficult for Glasgow, and only a handful of churches were constructed in the 1920s. The last United Free churches built in Glasgow were New Bridgegate, Crosshill (1923; no longer in use) and Hillington Park (1924–5), both in the mould of that denomination's prewar buildings. South Carntyne (**36**, 1937, Church of Scotland) is similar to Hillington Park in its architectural treatment.

The last church completed for the Church of Scotland which local landowners (heritors) paid for in the traditional way was Cathcart Old (**46**, 1914, 1923–9). In 1929, the United Free Church and the Church of Scotland came together as the Church of Scotland, partly to rationalise church provision. From then until the Second World War, several churches were built to serve new

Fig. 14. St Margaret's Parish Church, Great Western Road, Glasgow

housing areas. The last 'traditional' stone-faced buildings to be constructed before the Second World War were St Enoch Hogganfield (1927–30), South Carntyne (see above), the more adventurous St John Renfield (**29**, 1929–30) and St Margaret's, Knightswood (1929-32, Fig. 14) – notable, and very different, late Arts and Crafts buildings. The other Church of Scotland buildings of the 1930s were products of Church Extension. King's Park (**44**, 1934), a brick Romanesque building, was constructed as a prototype for such churches. The style was used for several other churches of the period, such as Calton Parkhead (1934–5), Croftfoot (**45**, 1934–6), and Trinity Possil and Henry Drummond (1934–6). The Mure Memorial Church, Baillieston (1936–40) is a variant on this style, and so, too, is St David's Knightswood (1938–9). Drumchapel Old (1936–9; now Drumchapel St Andrew's), white-harled, with stone dressings, is low-key Arts and Crafts. The Roman Catholic Church began a long connection with Gillespie, Kidd & Coia in the 1930s, their first church being St Anne's, Dennistoun (1931-3), a low brick-faced building with a concrete dome. Their much larger St Columba's, Hopehill Road (**33**, 1937–41) has a dramatic interior with arched reinforced-concrete portal frames.

The Second World War again brought church-building to a halt (apart from small hall-churches at Blawarthill and Househillwood, completed in 1940), but more than eighty churches were built between the late 1940s and the early 1970s, mainly to serve new housing areas. At first, shortage of materials curbed new building. The first postwar churches in the city were St Brendan's Roman Catholic Church, Yoker (1949) and St Paul's Church of Scotland, Provanmill (1948-51), soon followed by Carnwadric and the initial hall-church at Priesthill, both opened in 1952. These were all fairly basic. The removal of Pollokshields Titwood church to Pollok (as St James's, **59**) in 1951-3 was dictated by shortages of materials. Toryglen, also opened in 1953, was the first really original postwar design, by Gratton & McLean.

From the mid-1950s, the pace of church-building accelerated, and the Roman Catholics led the pace in numbers of churches built, in structural innovation

Fig. 15. St Margaret Mary's Roman Catholic Church, Dougrie Road, Glasgow

and in virtuosity of design. In 1955-7, T. S. Cordiner built two large churches with concrete A-frames. The first was St Brigid, Toryglen, then the larger The Immaculate Conception, Maryhill (now demolished). The typical Cordiner church was, however, more conventional. Examples include St Margaret Mary, Castlemilk (1956-7, Fig. 15) and Christ the King, Simshill (1960). Alexander McAnally was generally also fairly conventional in his designs, such as St Teresa of Lisieux, Possilpark (1960). Most conservative of all were Pugin & Pugin, whose last churches in the Glasgow area are St Ninian's, Knightswood and St Robert Bellarmine, Priesthill, both completed in 1959 and looking like interwar buildings. St Paul's, Whiteinch (1957-60), by Charles Gray of Reginald Fairlie & Partners, though externally traditional, has exceptional stained-glass windows. Charles Gray's Our Lady of Perpetual Succour, Broomhill (1962-5) is a small but striking A-frame building.

The outstanding architects for the Roman Catholic Church in the postwar period were, however, Gillespie, Kidd & Coia. The firm's early postwar buildings were fine but not notably innovative. St Joachim's, Carmyle (1957) was one of a series of 'economical' churches; and St Charles Borromeo, Kelvinside Gardens (**17**, 1960), with its exposed concrete frame, is striking but conventional in layout. St Paul the Apostle, Shettleston (**40**, 1959) has an imposing front to a fairly conventional body. After Isi Metzstein and Andy MacMillan joined the firm, they designed some of the outstanding postwar churches. The finest in Glasgow was probably St Benedict's, Drumchapel (1965-7; now demolished); but St Martin, Castlemilk (1959-61), Our Lady of Good Counsel, Dennistoun (**35**, 1965) and St Benedict's, Easterhouse (1962-5) are all very fine.

Interesting Church of Scotland buildings of the 1950s and 1960s include St Mark's, Drumchapel (1955-6), a modest but well-detailed design, Drumry St Mary (**32**, 1955-7), more overtly modernist, and the extraordinary boat-shaped Castlemilk West (1957-9, Fig. 16). By 1960, influenced by Metzstein and Macmillan, church designs were becoming more innovative. Church of Scotland examples include the slab-fronted

Fig. 16. Castlemilk West Church of Scotland, Carmunnock Road and Glenacre Terrace, Glasgow

Fig. 17. Partick South Church of Scotland, Dumbarton Road, Glasgow

Blawarthill (1960–4), the circular Lochwood (1963–4; now demolished), the wedge-shaped St Andrew, Penilee (1963–5) and the pyramidal Anderston Kelvingrove (1970–2). McAnally's circular St James the Great, Crookston (**60**, 1968), and St Oswald's Scottish Episcopal Church, King's Park (1966), also break out of traditional planning, as do the 'brutalist' Our Lady of Consolation, Govanhill (**55**, 1969–71) and St Gregory Barbarigo, Maryhill (**28**, 1971). By that time, the postwar boom in church-building had virtually ended – and, when church-building was resumed in the 1980s, both the funding and the appetite for architectural innovation had gone. The typical church of that period was a Fleming Buildings structure, with laminated timber frame, as at Springburn (1981), Sandyhills and St Rollox (both 1984) and Partick South (1988, Fig. 17).

North and South Lanarkshire

Lanarkshire was not notably prosperous in the medieval period. There was never an abbey in the county, and of priories near Blantyre (mid-thirteenth century) and at Lesmahagow (founded in 1144 by David I) there are only fragmentary remains. Lamington was rebuilt in 1721 and subsequently, but retains a fine twelfth-century doorway. The most complete remains of medieval churches in the county are St Mary's, Biggar (**103**, 1546), the choir of St Bride's Church, Bothwell (**105**, fifteenth century), part of Douglas Collegiate Church (fourteenth–sixteenth century, converted to a mausoleum) and Covington (now a house). Part of the former St Kentigern's Church, Lanark survives in its former churchyard, and in Rutherglen the tower of the medieval church (with a later slated steeple) still stands. At Carnwath, there is an elaborate burial aisle associated with a former collegiate church. Nor is there much surviving from the early post-Reformation period. Parts of Pettinain (**139**, 1696), Cumbernauld Old (**87**, 1659) and Dalserf (**116**, 1655) are seventeenth-century, as are portions of the roofless churches of Cambusnethan (c. 1650) and Quothquan. The most distinguished architecturally is the burial aisle (1656) that forms the south end of Walston Church. New Monkland Parish Church (**78**, 1697) has a unique stumpy steeple, a precursor of the 'Georgian steeples' of the later eighteenth and early nineteenth centuries.

The county shared in the agricultural improvement of the eighteenth century, but its climate and terrain were ill-suited to arable farming. The first major eighteenth-century church was Hamilton Old (**122**, 1734), but the money to build it probably came from other parts of the Duke of Hamilton's large estates. It is an exceptional church for its period, designed by the leading Scots architect of the day, William Adam. Cairngryffe (**112**, 1750) was substantially remodelled in the early twentieth century but is recognisable as a typical eighteenth-century T-plan church. It was not until the 1770s that more churches were built, probably on account of the expansion of handloom weaving. Two new churches were built in Strathaven: Avendale Old Parish (**144**, 1774) and the East (Secession) Church (**145**, 1777). St Nicholas's Parish Church, Lanark (**131**) was constructed in 1774 (to replace St Kentigern's; see above), as was East Kilbride Old (tower added in 1816). The body of New Monkland Parish Church (**78**) was rebuilt on a larger scale in 1777. In 1781–2, a new church at Douglas replaced the use of the former collegiate church, and in 1789 the little church of Dolphinton (now Black Mount, **117**) was completed. The Secessions were strong in Lanarkshire, and in 1791 East Kilbride West was built as a Relief church. In 1799, a new church was built in Carluke (St Andrew's, **110**, since much modified). The first church in Lanarkshire with a classical steeple was Carstairs (1794). It was followed by Lesmahagow Old Church (**137**), constructed in 1803 to replace the former priory church. It was enlarged in 1810. Libberton (**138**, 1812) and Glasford (**121**, 1820) also have classical spires. The Secession churches of Strathaven East (**145**) and St Andrew's Bellshill had classical spires added in the 1840s. Culter (**115**, 1810) has a pleasing bellcote, but this may not be original. Kilsyth Burns and Old (**90**, 1816) is an early, and for Lanarkshire rare, example of a 'Heritors' Gothic' church.

From the 1820s, Lanarkshire began to prosper through the exploitation of its coal and ironstone. Airdrie also expanded its

Fig. 18. Kirk o' Shotts Parish Church, North Lanarkshire

Fig. 19. Lesmahagow Abbeygreen Parish Church, South Lanarkshire

cotton-weaving industry. The first large new church built in the 1820s was Kirk o' Shotts (1820, Fig. 18), a landmark early Gothic Revival building. Another large new Gothic Revival church was added to the choir of the medieval church at Bothwell (105) in 1833. In the following year, the classical West Parish Church (now New Wellwynd) was built in Airdrie, and in 1835 the classical St John's, Hamilton (124) was built to cater for the expanding population of the town. In the same year, Strathaven West (146) was built as a Relief church, in Tudor style. In 1836, a Relief church was also built in Hope Street, Lanark (now offices). Clarkston Parish Church, to the east of Airdrie, was built in 1837 to serve a new mining area, as was Wishaw Old. In Airdrie, the High Church of Scotland and the Reformed Presbyterian Church were both opened in 1838. In 1839, two innovative buildings were opened, in Airdrie and Coatbridge. St Margaret's Roman Catholic Church (80) was the first Roman Catholic church built in the county since the Reformation. It is in a simple classical style, but Gartsherrie Parish Church (now St Andrew's, 85) is one of the first steepled Gothic Revival churches in Scotland. It was built by the town's leading firm of ironmasters, Bairds of Gartsherrie. Cambuslang Old (107, 1841) is similar in scale and massing, but in Romanesque style. The second Roman Catholic church in the county was the Gothic St Mary's, Hamilton (129, 1846-7). The emergence of the Free Church at the Disruption of 1843 did not

Fig. 20. Rutherglen West Parish Church, South Lanarkshire

immediately have a dramatic effect in the area, but an early Free Church was Lesmahagow Abbeygreen (1844, Fig. 19). Probably the first large Free church in the county was Rutherglen West (1848–50, Fig. 20), a tall building with a Gothic tower. The former Wellwynd Church, Airdrie, was one of the first churches built by the United Presbyterian Church after its formation in 1847.

Between 1839 and 1851, a new church was built at Cambusnethan, near Wishaw, to replace the seventeenth-century building (see above). An early Scottish Episcopal church in the area is Christ Church, Lanark (**133**, 1853), like St Athanasius Roman Catholic Church, Carluke (**111**, 1857), a small simple building. The iron-working communities of Chapelhall and Calderbank, south of Airdrie, gained their simple Gothic churches in 1857 and in about 1860 respectively. Two distinctive churches of the 1860s are Auchengray (**102**, 1863), with a gable in the distinctive version of Gothic favoured by the Edinburgh architect F. W. Pilkington, and St Ignatius Roman Catholic Church, Wishaw (**101**), also idiosyncratic Gothic. Carnwath Parish Church (**113**, 1867) is a Gothic Revival rendering of an early nineteenth-century galleried rectangular church. It, and the United Presbyterian church at Kirkmuirhill (**130**, 1868), are each distinguished by a steeple. Altogether grander is the former St Leonard's Church of Scotland, Lanark (1867), with a notable spire. In 1870, Garturk Church (now Calder) in Whifflet was built to serve local miners, and this was followed by Dunbeth, Coatbridge (1872; now flats), Coats, Coatbridge (1874; recently closed) and Flowerhill, Airdrie (**79**, 1874). All of these are Gothic Revival except Flowerhill, which is in an elaborate Italian Romanesque style. Biggar Moat Park (1875, United Presbyterian; now a museum, Fig. 21) is in a simpler Romanesque style. Coats has a remarkable open tower – a notable landmark.

Though there was never the need for large numbers of large churches in Lanarkshire that there was in the cities, a few continued to be constructed, including Blantyre Old (1872), Biggar Gillespie (1873; now a community centre), Dalziel North, Motherwell (**93**, 1874; now Dalziel St Andrew's),

Fig. 21. The former Moat Park Church of Scotland, Biggar, South Lanarkshire

Fig. 22. Glencaple Parish Church, Abington, South Lanarkshire

Bargeddie (1876), Wishaw Thornlie (1876, United Presbyterian; now closed), Bellshill West (1878), Chryston (1878–9), Hamilton West (**123**, 1880, Free), Crosshill, Motherwell (1881, United Presbyterian) and St Mary's Roman Catholic, Lanark (**134**, 1908) – all Gothic Revival, with notable steeples. Greyfriars, Lanark (**132**, 1875, United Presbyterian), Wishaw Chalmers (1872, Free; now Wishaw South) and Kilsyth Anderson (Free) are more modest, but pleasing. Cadzow, Hamilton (**127**, 1875), a fine Gothic church, never received its intended steeple. Another large church of the period is Paterson United Free Church, Stonehouse (**143**, 1879), with an unusual crown steeple. The most striking church of the period is probably Livingstone Memorial, Blantyre (1880–2, United Presbyterian). St Ninian's Parish Church, Stonehouse (1896), with its crenellated tower, is more conventional but an impressive design. Most of the many other churches built in Lanarkshire in the later nineteenth century were fairly small. Examples include Overtown (**98**, 1876), Our Lady and St John's Roman Catholic, Blackwood (**104**, 1880), Lowther, Leadhills (**136**, 1883, Free), Douglas Water (**140**, 1886, Free), St Andrew's Scottish Episcopal, Uddingston (**150**, 1890) and Glencaple, Abington (late 1890s, Fig. 22).

The other large churches in the area built in the 1890s and early 1900s are the Roman Catholic churches designed by Pugin & Pugin and also built to similar designs in Glasgow, Dunbartonshire and Stirlingshire. The first of the Lanarkshire examples is St Mary, Whifflet (1893), followed by St Aloysius, Chapelhall (**84**, 1894), St Patrick, Coatbridge (**86**, 1896), St Patrick, Shieldmuir (1898), St Augustine, Langloan (1899), Our Lady of Good Aid, Motherwell (1900; now cathedral), St Patrick, Shotts (**99**) and St Joseph, Blantyre (both 1905). At first glance, these churches look remarkably uniform – but their detailed differences repay examination.

Church-building in Lanarkshire tailed off after 1900, but some interesting buildings were constructed in the early twentieth century. These included the United Free Cambusnethan North (1903) and Hamilton Baptist (1908–9), both relatively small, and the former St Andrew's, Motherwell (1909; now Calvary Church), a compressed Scots Gothic building. Stonelaw, Rutherglen (1910–12, United Free) is a good example of the style of church favoured by that denomination in the years following its formation in 1900. In complete contrast is the former Dalziel North United Free Church, Motherwell (1915; now a gospel church). Its tall Romanesque campanile dominates the town centre. Drumclog Memorial Church (**119**, 1912), on the edge of South Lanarkshire, is an unusual essay in late Scots Gothic. The only First World War church in the area is St Mary's Church of Scotland, Motherwell (1918), a late and fine example of the early twentieth-century Romanesque Revival.

The interwar years were not kind to Lanarkshire, with the Lanarkshire coalfield nearing exhaustion, and the traditional iron and steel industries suffering from low levels of demand. Many people emigrated or moved south to Corby, Northamptonshire to work in the new steel works and tube mill built by the Lanarkshire firm Stewarts & Lloyds in the early 1930s. Only tiny churches at Tarbrax (**149**, 1919) and Coalburn (**114**, 1922) were built in the county until the end of the period, when Gillespie, Kidd & Coia's remarkable modernist, monumental St Columbkille's Roman Catholic Church, Rutherglen (**142**) was constructed. It was not finished until 1940.

After the war, the drive to build homes fit for heroes, and to rehouse people living in slum conditions, created a new demand for churches. All the larger towns in the county built new housing areas, and in addition the New Towns of East Kilbride and Cumbernauld were established, primarily to house people from Glasgow. The Church of Scotland's Church Extension scheme and a comparable Roman Catholic initiative resulted in the building of unprecedented numbers of new churches. Minority denominations also built churches, some of considerable interest. Early churches were fairly traditional, like Corpus Christi Roman Catholic Church, Calderbank (**82**, 1952). St Mark's Scottish Episcopal Church, East Kilbride (1956, Fig. 23) is a very

Fig. 23. St Mark's Scottish Episcopal Church, East Kilbride, South Lanarkshire

Fig. 24. St Anthony's Roman Catholic Church,
Mar Gardens, Burnside, South Lanarkshire

handsome example of the then-fashionable A-frame design. A good example of a Church of Scotland church of the period is Hillhouse (**126**, 1955). The mould of postwar church design was broken by Gillespie, Kidd & Coia's St Paul's, Glenrothes, Fife – and a succession of innovative designs followed. The practice's work in our area is challenging. St Bride's Roman Catholic Church, East Kilbride (**120**, 1964) is an uncompromising brick structure, impressive even after losing its campanile; and St Patrick's Roman Catholic Church, Kilsyth (**91**, 1963) and the Sacred Heart, Cumbernauld (1964) are scarcely less innovative. There are other interesting modernist churches in Lanarkshire, including St Anthony, Burnside (1967–70, Fig. 24), St Francis Xavier, Carfin (**83**, 1973), St Bride, Bothwell (**106**, 1973) and St Stephen, Sikeside, Coatbridge (1975–6), all Roman Catholic buildings. In Cumbernauld, there are two good Church Extension churches, St Mungo's (1964–6) and Kildrum (1962), both by Alan Reiach. The most striking of the East Kilbride Church Extension buildings are the polygonal South (1964) and Claremont (1971) churches. One of the most recent churches in the area is St David of Scotland Roman Catholic Church, Plains (1994).

East Dunbartonshire

This small local-authority area curves round the north and east sides of Glasgow. Part of it is rural, and there are six sizeable communities: Bearsden, Bishopbriggs, Lennoxtown, Lenzie, Milngavie and Kirkintilloch, as well as a number of smaller places. Lenzie, Bearsden and Bishopbriggs have, since their foundation in the mid- to late nineteenth century, always been essentially suburbs of Glasgow, but Lennoxtown, Milngavie and Kirkintilloch were until the late twentieth century largely industrial settlements. Now they, too, are primarily dormitories for Glasgow. Kirkintilloch is the oldest community and has the oldest church in the area. The Auld Kirk (1644) is a very fine example of a Greek Cross-plan church, typical of the Church of Scotland for most of the seventeenth century. It is now a museum. Baldernock (**66**, 1795) is the next oldest – a fine building, unusually with a symmetrical plan. Built as a country church, it is still in a rural setting. New

Kilpatrick (**67**) must have been a country church when it was first built in 1807. Cadder (**70**, 1825), a typical 'Heritors' Gothic' church with pinnacled tower, is still, remarkably, in a rural setting. Lennoxtown's old parish church was replaced in the 1980s by the present Campsie Parish Church (**73**). Its Roman Catholic church of St Machan (1846) is an early one. Milngavie acquired its first Church of Scotland church in 1838 (now a house). The active Church of Scotland churches are Cairns (**75**, 1903, formerly United Free), St Paul's (1898), both late Gothic Revival, and the modern St Luke's and Bearsden North; the Roman Catholic church was formerly a Free church.

The development of railways profoundly affected the area. Lenzie was developed by the railway companies as a middle-class suburb, large enough by the 1870s to justify building three churches. Lenzie Old (Church of Scotland) and St Cyprian's Scottish Episcopal Church (**74**) both date from 1873, and Lenzie Union (United Presbyterian, product of an agreement between that church and the Free Church as to which should build in Lenzie) was added in 1875. Bearsden and Milngavie were both linked to Glasgow in 1863. The existing New Kilpatrick church was extended on several occasions, and new churches were added in 1873–4 and 1887 by the United Presbyterian and Free churches. Bearsden South, the former Free church, was destroyed by bombing in 1941, and a new church was put up on the site in the 1950s. Bearsden North is no longer in use for worship. The little Scottish Episcopal church, All Saints, was put up as a temporary building in 1897 but is still in use. In the 1950s, Church Extension churches were built at Killermont (**68**, where there had been a hall since 1935) and Westerton (Fairlie Memorial). Both opened in 1957. The modernist Roman Catholic church of St Andrew dates from 1987 (Fig. 25).

Kirkintilloch had some suburban development but was primarily industrial. Its older churches are the Roman Catholic Church of the Holy Family and St Ninian (1893), a typical Pugin & Pugin building; St Mary's Parish Church (1914, Church of Scotland); and St David's Memorial

Fig. 25. St Andrew's Roman Catholic Church, Roman Road, Bearsden, East Dunbartonshire

Fig. 26. Bishopbriggs Kenmure Parish Church,
East Dunbartonshire

Park (**71**, 1926). In the later twentieth century, churches were built to serve new housing areas, Hillhead and St Columba's (1969) for the Church of Scotland and St Flannan's (**72**, 1970) for the Roman Catholic Church. Bishopbriggs had a station on the Edinburgh and Glasgow Railway from its opening in 1842, but its real growth dates from the early twentieth century. Bishopbriggs Kenmure Church of Scotland dates from 1905 (originally United Free, Fig. 26), and the other churches date from the mid- to late twentieth century. St Matthew's Roman Catholic church (1950) is one of a number of 'economical' postwar buildings designed by Gillespie, Kidd & Coia. The construction of Springfield Cambridge Church of Scotland (1972) was largely financed from compensation for the loss of Cambridge Street church, Glasgow, paid to the Church by Glasgow Corporation. Another Roman Catholic church, St Dominic's Woodhill, was added in 1977, and in 1980 St James the Less (**69**), one of the few postwar churches built by the Scottish Episcopal Church, was opened.

Outside the suburban area is Twechar, a coal-mining settlement. The Parish Church was built in 1902, financed by the owners of the pits, William Baird & Co. A Roman Catholic church, St John of the Cross, was added in 1969.

East Renfrewshire

This area was entirely rural until the late eighteenth century when water-powered cotton-spinning mills were established in Eaglesham, in Busby, in Neilston and in what became Barrhead. There are three churches in the area dating, at least in part, from the eighteenth century. Neilston (**163**, 1746) was enlarged in 1798 to accommodate cotton workers brought into the village. Mearns (**165**) dates in part from 1755 but was partly rebuilt in 1813 and again in 1932. The steeples of these two churches, with ogee caps, are unusual and fine. Eaglesham (**157**) was built in 1790, originally on an octagonal plan, with a classical steeple.

Because the area was largely rural, apart from the cotton-mill settlements, the Disruption of 1843 had little effect. Bourock Church, Barrhead, was being built as a Chapel of Ease for Neilston during the Disruption, but Barrhead Free (now South) was constructed soon after (1846). The little Roman Catholic church of St Bridget, Eaglesham (**158**) was completed in 1858, followed in 1861 by St Thomas, Neilston (**163**, tower added in 1891).

In the later nineteenth and the twentieth centuries, the northern and eastern parts of the area became suburbs of Glasgow, and most of the churches built since 1880 have been essentially for suburban areas. The first were the Gothic Greenbank, Clarkston (**153**, 1884) and Caldwell (**167**, 1889), serving the outer suburb of Uplawmoor. Orchardhill, Giffnock (**159**, 1900) is an outstanding Arts and Crafts church in a select suburb. Giffnock South (**160**, 1921–9) and Netherlee (**161**, 1934) are late examples of sandstone church buildings, with ample hall provision attached to a simply-detailed church. St Aidan's Scottish Episcopal Church, Clarkston (**154**) started as a hall-church in 1924; a church was added in 1951. Newton Mearns (1939) is a late and less sophisticated example of the type. In contrast, Williamwood (**168**, 1937) is a typical Church Extension building in brick, in a simple Romanesque Revival style.

Because the housing in the area was predominantly middle-class, there was not the density of church-building in the post-1945 period found in other parts of the west, but two Barrhead churches were rebuilt in modernist style: St John's Roman Catholic (**152**, 1961) is typical of the work of Thomas Cordiner, replacing a church destroyed by fire in 1941; and Arthurlie Church of Scotland (**151**, 1967) was a replacement for a church built in 1796. Four new buildings were constructed for the Church of Scotland between 1952 and 1974. Giffnock The Park started as a hall-church in 1952; a church proper was added later. Stamperland (**155**), too, started as a hall-church – the church proper was completed in 1964. Broom (**164**) opened in 1959. The most unusual is Maxwell Mearns Castle (**166**), built adjacent to a tower-house, which was used for a time as the church. The church proper, on a circular plan, opened in 1974. There is a pleasing little Gillespie, Kidd & Coia church (St Vincent de Paul, 1960) in Thornliebank. The most recent churches in the area are in Crookfur – St Cadoc's Roman Catholic Church (1981) and a large Baptist church.

Conclusion

Historically, there have been more churches in our area than anywhere else in Scotland – and there still are, though many have gone. The variety of approaches to church design taken by architects and congregations is readily apparent both from the gazetteer section and from this Introduction, making any pilgrimage through Glasgow and the Clyde Valley an interesting and stimulating one. What is not so obvious from what one can see today is the variety of spiritual journeys that have been undertaken which have resulted in the rich tapestry of church buildings that we can see around us. This Introduction has attempted to summarise some of the underlying complexity of the church history of the area, and of the socio-economic context in which it is set. More than in any other area of Scotland, it merely scratches the surface of a complex and intriguing set of buildings. Go and see them, and engage with the people who have inherited such a wide range of approaches to the worship of God. You will not be disappointed.

Professor John R. Hume
Universities of Glasgow and St Andrews

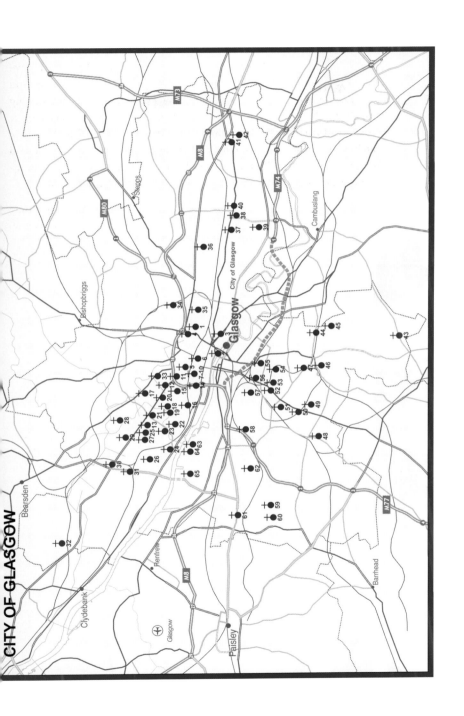

CITY OF GLASGOW

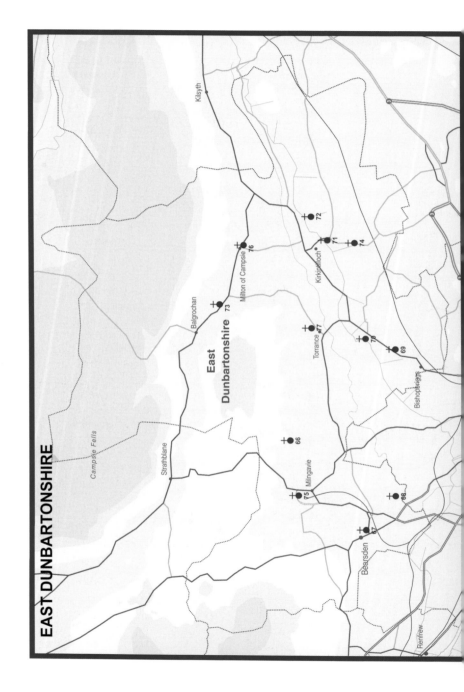

EAST DUNBARTONSHIRE

Kilsyth

Campsie Fells

Strathblane

Balgrochan

Milton of Campsie

East
Dunbartonshire

Kirkintilloch

Torrance

Milngavie

Bishopbriggs

Bearsden

Renfrew

72
71
74
76
73
77
70
69
66
75
68
67

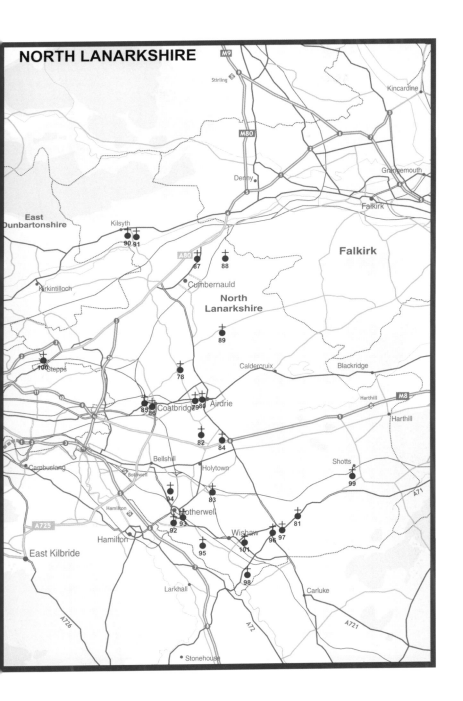

NORTH LANARKSHIRE

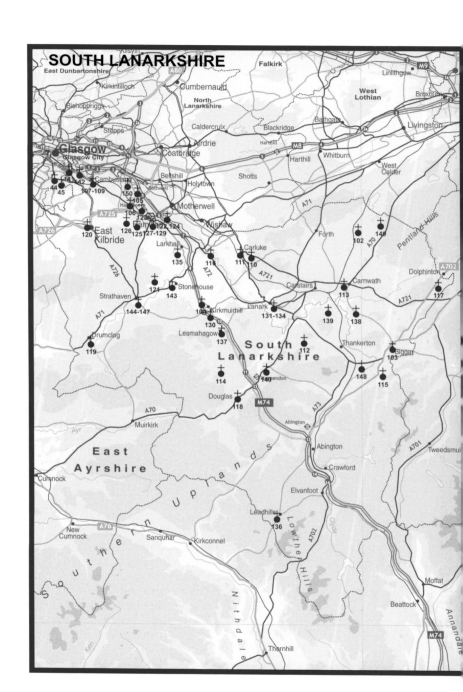

EAST RENFREWSHIRE

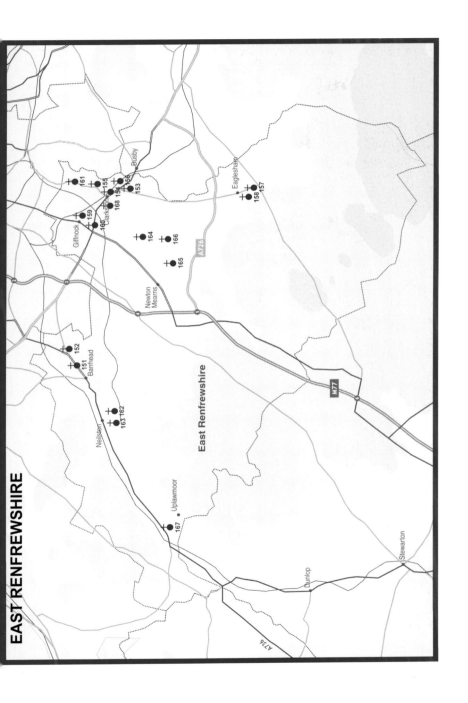

How to use this Guide

Entries are arranged by local-authority area, with large areas sub-divided for convenience. The number preceding each entry refers to the map. Each entry is followed by symbols for access and facilities:

⋏	Ordnance Survey reference	𝔇	Hearing induction loop for the deaf
▟	Denomination	👤	Welcomers and guides on duty
⊕	Church website		
●	Regular services	📖	Guidebooks and souvenirs available/for sale
○	Church events		Church Recorders' Inventory
●	Opening arrangements	NADFAS	(NADFAS)
♿	Wheelchair access for partially abled	☕	Refreshments
WC	Toilets available for visitors	🅐	Category A listing
WC	Toilets adapted for the disabled available for visitors	🅑	Category B listing
		🅒	Category C listing

Category A: Buildings of national or international importance, either architectural or historic, or fine little-altered examples of some particular period, style or building type.

Category B: Buildings of regional or more than local importance, or major examples of some particular period, style or building type which may have been altered.

Category C: Buildings of local importance, lesser examples of any period, style, or building type, as originally constructed or moderately altered; and simple traditional buildings which group well with others in categories A and B.

The information appearing in the gazetteer of this guide is supplied by the participating churches. While this is believed to be correct at the time of going to press, Scotland's Churches Scheme cannot accept any responsibility for its accuracy.

① CATHEDRAL CHURCH OF ST MUNGO

**Castle Street
Glasgow
G4 0QZ**

⚔ NS 603 656

⛪ Church of Scotland

🌐 www.glasgow-cathedral.com

Dedicated in 1136, the largest and most complete of Scotland's medieval cathedrals still in use. Medieval stone screen. Crypt with shrine of St Mungo. Outstanding collection of 20th-century glass by Francis Spear, Herbert Hendrie, Robert Armitage and Sadie McLellan, William Wilson, Gordon Webster, Harry Stammes and John K. Clark. Modern tapestry. Organ by Willis 1879, rebuilt by Harrison & Harrison 1996.

- Sunday: 11.00am and 6.30pm
- Open daily, April to September 9.30am–5.30pm, Sunday 1.00–5.00pm; October to March 9.30am–4.00pm, Sunday 1.00–4.00pm (0141 552 8198)

 (in St Mungo Museum)

② ST ANDREW'S METROPOLITAN CATHEDRAL

**Clyde Street
Glasgow
G1 4JY**

⚔ NS 592 647

⛪ Roman Catholic

🌐 www.cathedralg1.org

First major piece of Gothic Revivalism in Glasgow, by James Gillespie Graham, 1816. The façade has substantial buttresses either side of the ornate entrance and a statue of St Andrew above the large central window. Following its designation as a cathedral in 1884, the interior was renovated by Pugin & Pugin. Organ was originally in Elgin Place Congregational Church. Church closed for restoration until late 2010.

- While church is closed, Mass celebrated in Eyre Hall at the Curial Offices, 196 Clyde Street: Sunday: 10.00am and 12 noon, and Monday to Friday: 8.15am
- Open by arrangement (0141 221 3096)

ST ALPHONSUS CHURCH

**217 London Road
Glasgow
G40 2ST**

NS 600 646

Roman Catholic

www.stalphonsus.co.uk

500 metres east of Glasgow Cross

A late work by Peter Paul Pugin, 1905. Rock-faced sandstone screen façade. The tracery in the gable window formalised into a saltire cross. Inside, the nave arcades have polished granite piers. 150th-anniversary commemorative window 1996 by Lorraine Lamond. Church is in the middle of the 'Barras'.

- Saturday: Vigil 4.30pm; Sunday: 10.00am, 11.00am, 12.00 noon, 5.00pm
- Open Monday to Friday 12.00 noon–2.00pm, Saturday and Sunday 9.00am–6.00pm (0141 552 0519)

ST MUNGO'S CHURCH

**Parson Street
Glasgow
G4 0RX**

NS 600 659

Roman Catholic

www.saintmungo.org

Opposite Charles Rennie Mackintosh's Martyrs School

Designed by the London architect George Goldie 1869 in French Gothic style. High altar by Gillespie, Kidd & Coia 1952. The church is in the care of the Passionist congregation. Five apsidal chapels include St Paul of the Cross (founder of the Passionists), St Margaret of Scotland, and Our Lady of Sorrows, which has a Portuguese polychrome wood statue. Late 19th-century stained glass by Mayer of Munich. Gothic-style timber confessionals.

- Sunday: 10.00am, 12.00 noon and 7.00pm
- Open Monday to Friday 9.30am–1.00pm, 5.30–6.30pm; Saturday 9.30am–1.00pm, 4.30–8.00pm; Sunday 9.30am–1.00pm, 6.30–8.00pm (0141 552 1823)

GLASGOW

CITY CENTRE

5 ST ALOYSIUS CHURCH

**25 Rose Street
Glasgow
G3 6RE**

Λ NS 586 660

⛪ Roman Catholic

🌐 www.saint-aloysius.org.uk

Fine late-Renaissance-style church, designed in 1910 by Belgian-born architect Charles Menart, with a 46m (150ft) campanile, domed crossing and ornate marble-lined interior with painted ceiling. The church is in the care of the Jesuit Order, and Jesuit saints figure in the stained glass. The shrine of St John Ogilvie SJ is in the east transept, with mosaics depicting his martyrdom in Glasgow in 1615.

- Saturday: Vigil 5.45pm; Sunday: 9.00am, 10.30am (family), 12.00 noon (sung), and 9.00pm; weekdays: 8.00am, 12.30pm and 5.45pm
- Open Monday to Friday 7.30am–6.15pm, Saturday 9.00am–7.00pm, Sunday 8.30am–10.00pm (0141 332 3039)

6 ST GEORGE'S

Tron Parish Church

**165 Buchanan Street
Glasgow
G1 2JX**

Λ NS 590 655

⛪ Church of Scotland

🌐 www.thetron.org

Designed by William Stark and completed 1808. Originally St George's Parish Church and the eighth burgh church to be built in Glasgow in what was then the extreme west end of the city. St George's united with Tron St Anne's in 1940. Baroque-style tower with five stages capped by a ribbed dome and obelisk. Plain, galleried interior with flat ceiling. The Christ-centred life and ministry of Rev. Tom Allan (1955–64) was instrumental in the awakening of the evangelical Christian church in Glasgow and beyond.

- Sunday: 11.00am and 6.30pm; The 30-Minute Service each Wednesday 1.10–1.40pm; Wednesday Prayer Meeting 1st and 3rd Wednesday of each month; House Groups 2nd and 4th Wednesday of each month
- Open Monday to Saturday 10.00am–4.00pm (0141 332 2795)

7 RENFIELD ST STEPHEN'S PARISH CHURCH

**260 Bath Street
Glasgow
G2 4JP**

NS 582 659

Church of Scotland

www.rsschurch.net

Designed as an Independent Chapel by London architect J. T. Emmett in 1852 in Decorated Gothic style. Built in beautiful polished Kenmure sandstone with tall clerestoried nave supported on columns with finely carved musical angels. Evangelists windows by Norman Macdougall 1905, and representations of Christian virtues, flanking Christ in Glory. A church centre with side chapel, offices, extensive halls and restaurant was added in the 1960s. Patio with fountain from Glasgow Garden Festival. Following the collapse of the steeple during a storm on St Stephen's Day 1998, the church and basement have been sensitively restored and modernised.

- Sunday: 11.00am; Wednesday: 1.00pm
- Open Monday to Saturday 10.00am–6.00pm (0141 332 4293)

     (Oasis Café)

8 GLASGOW QUAKER MEETING HOUSE

**38 Elmbank Crescent
Glasgow
G2 4PS**

NS 581 656

Quaker

www.quakerscotland.gn.apc.org/glasgow

There has been a Quaker Meeting House in Glasgow since 1660. The present Meeting House was opened in 1993 in this two-storey-and-basement classical townhouse with balustraded parapet.

- Sunday 11.00am; Wednesday: 12.30pm, with simple shared lunch
- Open by arrangement (0141 248 8493)

9 ST VINCENT STREET CHURCH

Milton Free Church

265 St Vincent Street
Glasgow
G2 5RL

⚑ NS 583 656

⛪ Free Church of Scotland

🌐 www.greekthomsonchurch.com

Alexander Thomson's masterpiece, a distinctive Victorian Presbyterian church of 1859, designed in the style of a classical temple on a plinth, and embellished by a unique Thomsonian combination of Egyptian, Indian and Assyrian influences. The tower grows ever more elaborate towards its top. The lofty church interior is wonderfully rich and colourful. Owned by Glasgow City Council.

- Sunday: 11.00am and 6.30pm
- Open by arrangement (0141 959 2385)

10 ADELAIDE PLACE BAPTIST CHURCH

209 Bath Street
Glasgow
G2 4HZ

⚑ NS 584 658

⛪ Baptist

🌐 www.adelaides.co.uk

Built 1877, architect T. L. Watson, when the congregation moved from Hope Street. Classical façade with Corinthian columns supporting the pediment. Stained glass by W. & J. J. Keir. Award-winning redevelopment in 1995 by Gillespies saw the founding of 'Adelaide's' and the creation of a multi-functional centre including sanctuary, guest house and nursery. The church has a ministry to businesses in Glasgow.

- Sunday: 11.00am
- Open Monday to Saturday 9.00am–6.00pm, except when sanctuary is in use. Telephone first to check (0141 248 4970)

11 GARNETHILL SYNAGOGUE

**129 Hill Street
Glasgow
G3 6UB**

NS 502 661

Jewish

Off Garnet Street

Opened in 1879, the first purpose-built synagogue in Scotland. It was designed by John McLeod of Glasgow in Romanesque-cum-Byzantine style. A round-arched portal with highly decorated orders leads to the body of the synagogue. Ladies' gallery is carried on octagonal piers with ornate Byzantine capitals. Stained glass by J. B. Bennet & Sons. Refurbished in 1996.

- Saturday: 10.00am, Jewish festivals: 9.30am
- Open by arrangement (0141 332 4151)

12 ST MARY'S EPISCOPAL CATHEDRAL

**300 Great Western Road
Glasgow
G4 9JB**

NS 578 668

Scottish Episcopal

www.thecathedral.org.uk

Fine Gothic Revival church in Early English style by Sir George Gilbert Scott, 1871; the 61m (200ft) spire was added in 1893. The chancel was refitted by Sir Robert Lorimer after the Great War. The high altar reredos by Lorimer has paintings by Phoebe Anna Traquair. Outstanding murals of 1998 by Gwyneth Leech. Three-manual pipe organ. Glasgow's only full peal of bells. Major restoration 2002.

- Sunday: Eucharist 8.30am, Sung Eucharist 10.30am, Choral Evensong 6.30pm; weekdays: 9.30am morning prayer, Thursday 11.00am Eucharist
- Open by arrangement (0141 339 6691)

13 CATHEDRAL CHURCH OF ST LUKE

**27 Dundonald Road
Dowanhill
Glasgow
G12 9LL**

⚔ NS 563 675

🏛 Orthodox

🌐 www.stluke.org.uk

Formerly Belhaven United Presbyterian Church by James Sellars 1877, powerfully vertical Normandy Gothic. The congregation of St Luke's relocated here in 1960. The main front is inspired by Dunblane Cathedral. Marvellous display of stained glass, Stephen Adam 1877, richly stencilled roof timbers, and original light fittings and furniture. Modern iconostasis featuring icons, some of which were painted on Mount Athos in the traditional Byzantine style.

- Sunday: 10.30am–1.00pm
- Open by arrangement (0141 339 7368)

14 ST PATRICK'S, ANDERSTON

**137 William Street
Glasgow
G3 8UR**

⚔ NS 580 655

🏛 Roman Catholic

🌐 www.stpatsanderston.org.uk

Designed by Pugin & Pugin in early Decorated style, and opened for worship in 1898. One of the most striking of the many features within the church is the high altar of white marble, supported on six columns of Connemara marble with floreated capitals. The throne is surmounted by a magnificent cupola of Caen stone.

- Saturday: 6.00pm; Sunday: 10.00am and 12.00 noon; various daily services
- Open daily 8.00am–5.00pm, except Wednesday open 8.00am–12 noon (0141 221 3579)

15 WOODLANDS METHODIST CHURCH

**229 Woodlands Road
Glasgow
G3 6LW**

⚲ NS 576 665

⛪ Methodist

🌐 www.woodlandsmethodistchurch.
   org.uk

Linked with Shettleston Methodist
Church (37)

Built for Swedenborgians by David
Barclay, 1909, and in use by the
Methodists since 1977. A wide stair
leads to the church. Organ 1876 from
Cathedral Street Swedenborgian
Church, originally built by Forster &
Andrews and augmented with pipes
from the Willis organ at St John's,
Sauchiehall Street. Windows by
Guthrie & Wells and George Benson,
and war-memorial window from St
John's.

- Sunday: 11.00am
- Open by arrangement (0141 639 9436)

16 SANDYFORD HENDERSON CHURCH

**13 Kelvinhaugh Street
Glasgow
G3 8NU**

⚲ NS 571 659

⛪ Church of Scotland

🌐 www.sandyfordhenderson.net

Early Gothic-style 1855 by J. T.
Emmett, completed by John
Honeyman. Fine stained-glass aisle
windows in geometric/floral patterns
by Ballantine & Allan, Edinburgh 1857,
and three pictorial west windows by
William Wailes, Newcastle 1859–60.
First World War memorial chancel
added 1922. Exterior stonework
restored 2000; interior refurbishment
2004. Chancel window screen by
Margaret Craig, 2004. Complete
restoration of stained glass, 2008–9.

- Sunday: 11.00am and 6.30pm;
  Wednesday: 7.30pm Prayer and Bible
  Study
- Open Wednesday 10.00am–12.00
  noon or by arrangement (0141 886
  5871)

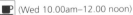 (Wed 10.00am–12.00 noon)

17 ST CHARLES BORROMEO

**1 Kelvinside Gardens
Glasgow
G20 6BG**

Ⲁ NS 576 676

🏛 Roman Catholic

Designed by Andy MacMillan and
Isi Metzstein of Gillespie, Kidd &
Coia for a tight, steep hillside site
and built 1959–60. The most notable
internal features are the excellent
Benno Schotz sculptures: bronze altar
frontal, crucifix and lampholder and
12 terracotta Stations of the Cross
based on parishioners and friends of
Schotz.

- Saturday: Vigil 6.00pm; Sunday:
  11.00am, 6.00pm; Monday to
  Saturday: 10.00am
- Open 9.00–10.30am Monday to
  Saturday (0141 946 5950)

18 WELLINGTON CHURCH

**University Avenue
Glasgow
G12 8LE**

Ⲁ NS 570 667

🏛 Church of Scotland

🌐 www.wellingtonchurch.co.uk

T. L. Watson's Roman Classical church
with mighty Corinthian columned
portico 1884. Renaissance-style
interior with fine plaster ceilings. Pipe
organ Forster & Andrews. Refectory
situated in crypt.

- Sunday: 11.00am and 7.00pm
- Open Monday to Friday during
  University term; access via crypt
  (0141 339 0454)

19 UNIVERSITY MEMORIAL CHAPEL

The Square
Glasgow University
Glasgow
G12 8QQ

⚐ NS 568 666

🏠 Ecumenical

🌐 www.gla.ac.uk/chaplaincy

1923–7 by Sir J. J. Burnet in Scots Gothic and in harmony with the University buildings of Sir George Gilbert Scott. The structure is reinforced concrete, faced with stone. Tall interior with sculpture by Archibald Dawson. Ten of the stained-glass windows are by Douglas Strachan in a cycle depicting the whole of human life as a spiritual enterprise. Other windows by Gordon Webster and Lawrence Lee. The chapel incorporates the Lion and Unicorn Stair salvaged from the Old College.

- Sunday: 11.00am; Monday to Friday: 8.45am during term-time
- Open 9.00am–5.00pm Monday to Friday, 9.00am–12.00 noon Saturday (0141 330 5419)

 (Visitors' Centre)

20 LANSDOWNE PARISH CHURCH

416 Great Western Road
Glasgow
G4 9HZ

⚐ NS 576 669

🏠 Church of Scotland

🌐 www.thecottier.com/news.html?c=viewItem&id=30

On corner with Park Road, opposite Kelvinbridge Underground

Built 1863 to a design by John Honeyman. The spire of 66m (218ft), one of the slimmest in Europe, is a powerful landmark on Great Western Road. Box pews. Beautiful stained glass by Alfred and Gordon Webster, and war-memorial frieze by Evelyn Beale. Pipe organ 1911, Norman & Beard, said to have the finest tuba rank in Glasgow, with some wonderful flutes. Four Acres Charitable Trust is seeking funding for the restoration of this important church.

○ Closed for restoration; contact Four Acres Trust for information (0141 339 9407)

21 KELVINSIDE HILLHEAD CHURCH

**Saltoun Street
Glasgow
G12 9AD**

⋏ NS 567 673

🏠 Church of Scotland

🌐 www.kelvinside-hillhead.org.uk

Junction with Observatory Road, Dowanhill

1876 by James Sellars; design said to have been much influenced by William Leiper. A tall apsed church, with west front full of carving. Interior recast 1921 by Peter MacGregor Chalmers. Communion table of Rochette marble. Good stained glass by Burne-Jones for William Morris & Co. 1893 and Sadie McLellan 1958. Organ by H. Willis & Son 1876, restored 1930.

- Sunday: 11.00am all year and 6.30pm October to May
- Open Saturday 3.00–5.00pm or by arrangement (0141 334 2788)

22 ST SIMON'S, PARTICK

**33 Partick Bridge Street
Glasgow
G11 6PQ**

⋏ NS 563 664

🏠 Roman Catholic

🌐 www.stsimonspartick.org.uk

Founded by Daniel Gallagher, famous as 'the priest who taught David Livingstone Latin'. Built in Gothic style in 1858 by Charles O'Neill as St Peter's, renovated in 1956 by Gillespie, Kidd & Coia. Extensively refurbished 2005–8. Marble altar has a panel by Mortimer depicting Christ Comforted by His Mother. Used by the Polish community since the Second World War.

- Saturday: 6.00pm (Polish); Sunday: 10.00am (English), 12 noon (Polish), 6.00pm (English)
- Open daily 8.00am–6.00pm (0141 339 7618)

23 ST PETER'S, PARTICK

46–50 Hyndland Street Glasgow G11 5PS

Λ NS 561 668

Roman Catholic

🌐 www.stpeterspartick.co.uk

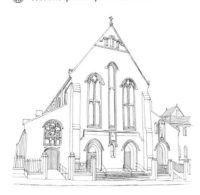

Substantial church by Peter Paul Pugin, 1903, in revived Gothic style. Bright interior lit by clerestory windows. Elaborate reredos. Pipe organ 1916, restored 1999. Good stained glass 1903 and 1937 plus pieces by Henry Clark from Dowanhill Convent. Redecorated for centenary celebrations 2003.

- Saturday: Vigil 6.00pm; Sunday: 10.00am (Polish), 12.00 noon (English) and 6.00pm (Polish); weekdays: 10.00am
- Open daily 9.00am–5.00pm (0141 357 5772)

24 PARTICK METHODIST CHURCH

524 Dumbarton Road Glasgow G11 6SN

Λ NS 553 666

Methodist

🌐 www.partickmethodistchurch.org.uk

Church and halls by W. F. McGibbon, opened 1881; celebrated its 125th anniversary in 2006. The gable facing the street has a three-light window above five small round-headed windows and a square tower alongside. Good stained glass by Abbot & Co. 1957. Fine organ by Forster & Andrews 1886, altered by H. Hilsdon around 1928.

- Sunday: 11.00am; occasional evening services
- Open by arrangement (0141 334 1181)

25 ST BRIDE'S, HYNDLAND

**69 Hyndland Road
Glasgow
G12 9UX**

⚔ NS 559 676

🏛 Scottish Episcopal

🌐 www.stbride.org.uk

Designed by G. F. Bodley, who built
the chancel 1904, the nave 1907 and
part of the north aisle. H. O. Tarbolton
completed the church (1913–16),
including rebuilding part of the nave
and adding two north aisles and the
tower. The interior scheme is mainly
Bodley's. Carved woodwork by Scott
Morton & Co. Sculpture of Our Lady
and Child by Eric Gill 1915. Very fine
2-manual organ by Hill 1865, installed
here 1972.

• Sunday: 10.30am, 3rd Sunday:
  3.30pm (not July or August); Monday
  and Wednesday: 5.30pm; Thursday:
  10.00am; 4th Saturday: 12.00 noon
• Open by arrangement (0141 334 1401)

26 BROOMHILL CHURCH

**64 Randolph Road
Glasgow
G11 7JL**

⚔ NS 549 674

🏛 Church of Scotland

🌐 www.broomhillchurch.org.uk

Junction with Marlborough Avenue

Red sandstone church 1902, and hall
1899, designed by Stewart & Paterson.
Stained glass by Guthrie & Wells,
Glasgow, Abbey Studio, Edinburgh
and Brian Hutchison. Pipe organ
refurbished by Harrison & Harrison
1997.

• Sunday: 11.00am and 6.30pm
• Open by arrangement (0141 334 2540)

27 HYNDLAND PARISH CHURCH

79 Hyndland Road Glasgow G12 9JE

🏹 NS 559 675

 Church of Scotland

🌐 www.hyndlandparishchurch.org

William Leiper 1887 in red Ballochmyle sandstone. Floodlit timber-vaulted interior roof, columns with richly carved capitals. Gleaming original terrazzo floor. Original furnishings, beautiful marble pulpit and common table, Henry Willis pipe organ, the whole building complemented by a collection of stained glass with windows by Norman Macdougall 1889, Douglas Strachan 1921, Douglas Hamilton 1930, Gordon Webster 1961, William Wilson 1962, Sax Shaw 1968, Paul Lucky 1984 and Rab MacInnes 1999. Additionally, three windows by Oscar Paterson 1897 moved here from St Bride's Church, Partick.

- Sunday: 11.00am and 6.30pm October to Palm Sunday; 10.30am Easter Day to September
- Open by arrangement (0141 334 1002)

28 ST GREGORY BARBARIGO

130 Kelvindale Road Glasgow G20 8DP

🏹 NS 565 686

 Roman Catholic

🌐 www.stgregorybarbarigo.co.uk

The church, dedicated to St Gregory Barbarigo, is strategically placed in the centre of the parish. The parish was founded in 1965 and the church, designed by Borthwick & Watson, was opened in 1971. The Kelvin walkway, which runs along the west side of the church, enhances the complex of buildings. One of the many attractive features of the church is the stained-glass Stations of the Cross.

- Saturday: Vigil 6.00pm; Sunday: 10.30am; weekdays: 9.30am
- Open every day 9.00–11.00am, Tuesday 9.00am– 7.00pm (0141 946 3009)

29 ST JOHN'S-RENFIELD

**Beaconsfield Road
Kelvindale
Glasgow
G12 0NY**

Å NS 558 683

  Church of Scotland

  www.stjohns-renfield.org.uk/
aboutUS.htm

Bold and striking church in a
commanding position. Topped by an
openwork flèche, the stonework has
the understated detail characteristic
of its time, 1931 (architect James
Taylor Thomson). Light and lofty
interior, complete with original
fitments, and stained glass by
Douglas Strachan and Gordon
Webster.

* Sunday: 11.00am
* Open April to October, Thursday
9.30am–12.30pm or by arrangement
(0141 334 0782)

30 TEMPLE-ANNIESLAND CHURCH

**869 Crow Road
Glasgow
G13 1LE**

Å NS 547 689

  Church of Scotland

Red sandstone Gothic-style church
built by Badenoch & Bruce 1905.
Adjoining hall was original United
Presbyterian church built in 1899 by
Alexander Petrie. U-plan interior with
red pine-panelled gallery and pews.
War Memorial, from Temple Parish
Church (now demolished), with
unique clock designed and built 1921
by its first minister, Rev. J. Carswell.

* Sunday: 11.00am and 6.30pm (July
and August 11.00am only); Thursday:
11.00am
* Open Thursday 10.00am–12.00 noon
(not July) (0141 959 1814)

31 JORDANHILL PARISH CHURCH

28 Woodend Drive Glasgow G13 1QT

NS 544 682

Church of Scotland

www.jordanhillparishchurch.org.uk

Off Crow Road (A739)

Church 1905 and hall, west aisle and gallery 1923 by James Miller in Perpendicular style. Battlemented and pinnacled tower. Mock hammerbeam roof spans the broad interior. Further extensions to hall 1971 and sanctuary refurbishment 1980 by Wylie Shanks. Organ by Lewis 1923.

- Sunday: 10.30am and 6.30pm, 1st Sunday of the month; Wednesday: 10.00am, September to June
- Open Monday to Friday 8.30am–12.30pm and 1.30–5.00pm (0141 959 2496)

32 DRUMRY ST MARY

217 Drumry Road East Drumchapel Glasgow G15 8NS

NS 515 709

Church of Scotland

Simple church (Ross, Doak & Whitelaw, 1955–7) with shallow-pitched roof, linked to hall by a vestibule with a bell turret. Contains a 120-year-old marble font from Old Partick Parish Church. Main feature is the Garden of Remembrance for Bereaved Parents as designed by and featured in BBC's *Beechgrove Garden*. Stones in the garden from the 'Peel of Drumry'.

- Sunday: 11.00am
- Church open weeknight evenings; garden open at all times, access via rear gate (0141 944 1998)

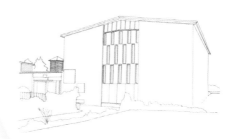

33 ST COLUMBA'S CHURCH

**74 Hopehill Road
Glasgow
G20 7HH**

NS 583 671

Roman Catholic

North of St George's Cross, via Maryhill Road

By Gillespie, Kidd & Coia, completed in 1941, the year of the Clydebank and Govan blitz. The cost was met by the families of the area, each of whom paid sixpence per brick. Italian Romanesque style with an imposing west front. Sculpture of the Paschal Lamb over central door. Painted panels of the Stations of the Cross by Hugh Adam Crawford, from the Catholic Pavilion at the Glasgow Empire Exhibition 1938. In the sanctuary, a marble reredos with a carved crucifix by Benno Schotz.

- Saturday: Vigil 6.00pm; Sunday: 11.00am and 5.00pm
- Open by arrangement (0141 332 4530)

34 ST ROCH

**311 Roystonhill
Glasgow
G21 2HN**

NS 612 665

Roman Catholic

www.strochs-garngad.org.uk

The church, designed by Walter R. Watson, was opened in 1907 to cater for the mainly Irish immigrants who had come to settle in the area. Nearby, there had been a chapel to St Roch built in 1506, but it was one of the casualties of the Reformation. The red-brick façade features a large window over the paired doors. Clerestory windows light the interior. Alterations were carried out in 1999 to enhance its simplicity and beauty.

- Saturday: Vigil 6.00pm; Sunday: 9.00 and 11.30am; weekdays: 10.00am
- Open on schooldays 9.00am–3.15pm (0141 552 2945)

35 OUR LADY OF GOOD COUNSEL, DENNISTOUN

**73 Craigpark
Dennistoun
Glasgow
G31 2JF**

NS 610 655

Roman Catholic

www.olgc.org.uk

Designed by Glasgow architects
Gillespie, Kidd & Coia, and opened in
1965. Features a dramatic tapering and
sloping copper-clad roof with deep
eaves. Inside, there is outstanding
brickwork and a high wooden ceiling.
Imposing altar.

- Saturday: Vigil 5.30pm; Sunday:
  10.00am, 12.00 noon, 5.30pm;
  weekdays: 10.00am
- Open 9.00–11.00am weekdays,
  9.00am–1.00pm and 5.00–6.00pm
  Sundays (0141 554 1558)

36 HIGH CARNTYNE PARISH CHURCH

**358 Carntynehall Road
Glasgow
G33 6LW**

NS 636 653

Church of Scotland

First 'church extension' charge of the
Church of Scotland. Congregation
met in 'the hut' until building was
completed by J. Taylor Thomson 1932.
Red-brick walls with stone windows
rise from stone base courses. Original
single bell still in use. Extensive suite
of halls built alongside the church
in 1955.

- Sunday: 11.00am; Wednesday: 9.30am
- Open by arrangement (0141 778 4186)

37 SHETTLESTON METHODIST CHURCH

**1104 Shettleston Road
Glasgow
G32 7PH**

⋏ NS 643 642

🏛 Methodist

🌐 www.shettlestonmethodist.co.uk

Linked with Woodlands Methodist
Church (15)

Opposite Shettleston Police Station

A church in the heart of the
community. This former Primitive
Methodist Church of 1902 replaced
a tin tabernacle of 1889. The church
incorporates windows from the
former Parkhead Methodist Church.

- Sunday: 11.00am; Tuesday: 10.30am
- Open by arrangement (0141 778 5063)

38 SHETTLESTON OLD PARISH CHURCH

**111 Killin Street
Shettleston
Glasgow
G32 9AH**

⋏ NS 649 640

🏛 Church of Scotland

🌐 www.shettlestonold.org.uk

Across Shettleston Road from
Shettleston Station

Church in red sandstone with slate
roofs by W. F. McGibbon, opened in
1903. A cluster of shapes, including
the hall and an entrance tower, leads
to the large nave. Fine collection of
stained glass, including windows by
Alfred Webster and Gordon Webster.
Fine 2-manual organ.

- Sunday: 11.00am
- Open by arrangement (0141 778 2484)

 (by arrangement)

ST JOSEPH'S, TOLLCROSS

**14 Fullarton Avenue
Tollcross
Glasgow
G32 8NJ**

A NS 644 631

Roman Catholic

www.rcag.org.uk/parishes_
stjoseph.htm

Built 1976 to replace a chapel school of 1893. Designed by Scott, Fraser & Browning. A dramatic copper roof covers a fan-shaped worship space lit by clerestory windows. Tapestry and embroidery by Netta Ewing of Sacred Threads.

- Saturday: Vigil 5.30pm; Sunday: 9.30am and 11.30am; weekdays: 9.30am
- Open daily 9.00am–11.00pm (0141 778 1054)

ST PAUL THE APOSTLE, SHETTLESTON

**1653 Shettleston Road
Glasgow
G32 9AR**

A NS 653 641

Roman Catholic

www.parishofsaintpauls.co.uk

Basilican church by Jack Coia 1959. Exterior copper calvary and Stations of the Cross by Jack Mortimer. Spacious interior with much marble and slate, reordered for modern liturgy. Interesting baptistry and a rebuilt organ from Greenlaw Parish Church, Paisley.

- Saturday: 5.30pm; Sunday: 10.00am, 11.30am and 6.30pm; Monday to Friday: 9.30am
- Open 7.30am–7.30pm (0141 778 1014)

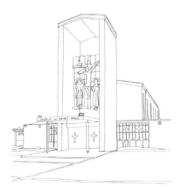

GLASGOW

EAST

41 ST BRIDGET'S, BAILLIESTON

**15 Swinton Road
Baillieston
Glasgow
G69 6DT**

NS 680 642

Roman Catholic

www.stbridgetsparish.com

200 metres west of Edinburgh Road/ Coatbridge Road

Built 1893 by Pugin & Pugin in light sandstone. Notable *Creation* rose window above sanctuary area and carved *Christ Triumphant* below. Mosaic work *Suffer the Children, Nativity, Glories of Mary, Annunciation*, and stained-glass windows *Christ with Saints* and *Sacred Heart* 1945–9 by the John Hardman Studios. *St Bridget* and *St Colmcille* windows by Shona McInnes 1999.

- Saturday: 5.30pm; Sunday: 9.00am, 10.30am, 12.00 noon and 6.00pm; Daily Service 9.30am
- Open for some hours each day or by arrangement (0141 771 1058)

42 BAILLIESTON ST ANDREW'S

Baillieston Parish Church

**2 Bredisholm Road
Baillieston
Glasgow
G69 7HL**

NS 681 639

Church of Scotland

www.standrewsbaillieston.org.uk

South side of Bredisholm Road at its junction with Church Street

Present church, by James Houston & Sons of Kilbirnie, was completed 1974 following the union of Baillieston Old and Rhinsdale Churches in 1966. Hexagonal design with a slim spire. Allen organ installed. A Bible-believing evangelical Presbyterian church.

- Sunday: 11.00am (all year) and 6.30pm (September to June); Wednesday: 7.30pm (September to June). Check the website for details of other services.
- Open by arrangement (0141 771 1791 or 0141 771 5120)

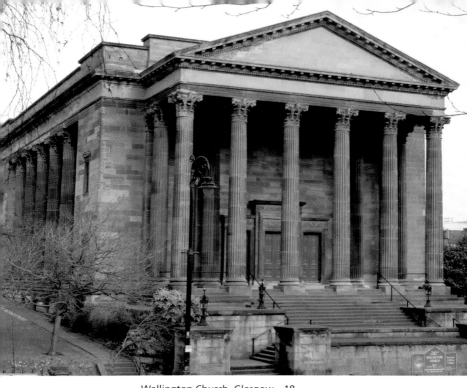

Wellington Church, Glasgow   18

Pettinain Church   139

Garnethill Synagogue, Glasgow   11

Renfield St Stephen's Parish Church, Glasgow   7

Glasgow Quaker Meeting House

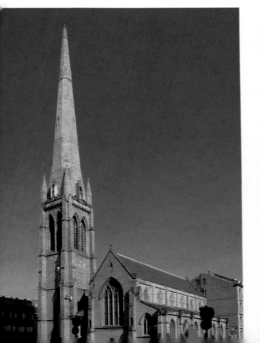

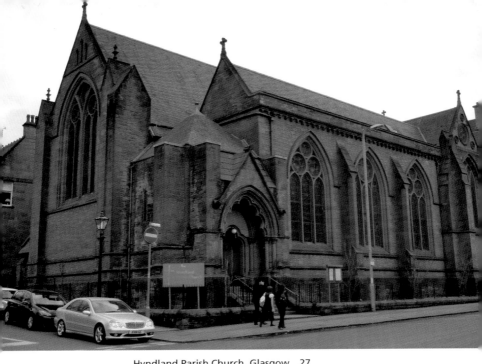

Hyndland Parish Church, Glasgow   27

St Vincent Street Church, Glasgow   9

St Mary's Episcopal Cathedral, Glasgow   12

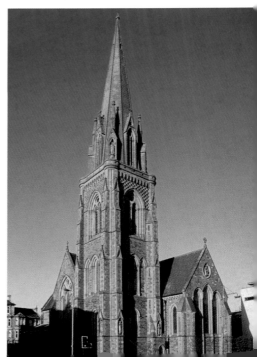

Biggar Kirk   103

Lansdowne Parish Church, Glasgow   20

St Bride's, Hyndland   25

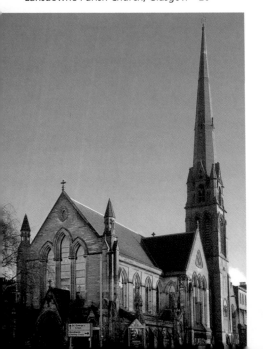

Dalserf Parish Church   116

St Aloysius Church, Glasgow   5

Mearns Parish Church, Newton Mearns   165

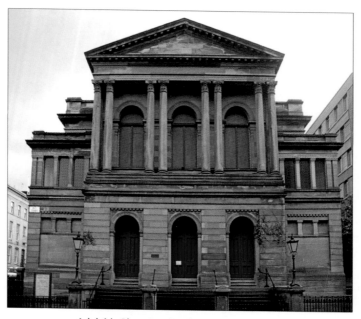

Adelaide Place Baptist Church, Glasgow 10

St Nicholas Parish Church, Lanark 131

St Bride's, East Kilbride 120

Govan and Linthouse Parish Church, Glasgow (Govan Old Building)   63

Bothwell Parish Church   105

Culter Parish Church, Coulter   115

St Paul the Apostle, Shettleston   40

Cathedral Church of St Mungo, Glasgow   1

St Columba's Church, Glasgow   33

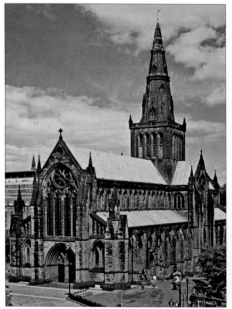

43 CARMUNNOCK PARISH CHURCH

The Kirk in the Braes

**Kirk Road
Carmunnock
G76 9DA**

 NS 599 575

Church of Scotland

Rebuilt 1767 on pre-Reformation site and repaired 1840. External stone staircases to three galleries. Laird's gallery. Stained glass by Norman Macleod MacDougall. Ancient graveyard has watch-house with original instructions for grave-watchers 1828, and burial vault of Stirling-Stuart family, Lairds of Castlemilk.

- Sunday: 11.00am
- Open April to September, Saturday 2.00–4.00pm or by arrangement (0141 644 1578)

44 KING'S PARK PARISH CHURCH

**242 Castlemilk Road
Glasgow
G44 2LB**

NS 601 608

Church of Scotland

www.kingsparkparishchurch.co.uk

Romanesque in style, by Hutton & Taylor 1932 in red brick with stone dressings. An innovation in church design specially evolved by the Presbytery of Glasgow through architectural competition. Notable collection of stained-glass windows by Sadie McLellan, Gordon Webster, Douglas Hamilton, Eilidh Keith and others. Set in a pleasant small garden. Floodlit as part of 'City of Light' project. Ample parking.

- Sunday: 11.00am all year, and 6.30pm July and August
- Open Monday to Friday 9.30am–12.00 noon all year, except public holidays. Tours by arrangement (0141 637 2803)

GLASGOW

SOUTH

45 CROFTFOOT PARISH CHURCH

**318 Croftpark Avenue
Glasgow
G44 5NS**

Å NS 603 602

⛪ Church of Scotland

🌐 www.croftfootparish.co.uk

A neat Byzantine design in red brick with ashlar facings by Keppie & Henderson 1936. Carved patterns, symbolising scriptural themes, decorate the main door portico, nave and chancel columns and chancel furnishings. The bell is the Second World War Memorial.

• Sunday: 11.00am and 6.30pm
• Open Monday to Friday 9.00am–12.00 noon, and 1.30–4.00pm, except public holidays (0141 637 3913)

46 CATHCART OLD PARISH CHURCH

**119 Carmunnock Road
Glasgow
G44 5UW**

Å NS 587 606

⛪ Church of Scotland

Original design 1923 by Clifford & Lunan, but completed 1928 by Watson, Salmon & Gray. The size is enhanced by the low porch and range of vestries. South transept contains a display of the church's history over 800 years; the north transept was converted in 1962 to the McKellar Memorial Chapel. Tapestry of *The Last Supper* by Charles Marshall; stained glass by James Crombie. Organ by John R. Miller 1890, restored and converted to electromechanical action 1994.

• Sunday: 11.00am
• Open Monday to Friday 10.00am–2.00pm (0141 633 5248)

 (The Haven: Mon to Fri 10.00am–1.30pm, Sun 12.00 noon–1.00pm)

GLASGOW

47 BATTLEFIELD EAST PARISH CHURCH

1220 Cathcart Road Glasgow G42 9EU

 NS 586 613

Church of Scotland

www.battlefieldeastchurch.com

Near Mount Florida railway station

The first church on this site was by John Honeyman 1865 in Early English style. It became the hall in 1912 when the adjacent red sandstone church by John Galt was opened. Spacious yet warm and intimate interior with galleries supported on cast-iron columns. Fine woodwork, especially the gallery fronts and wagon roof. Light plaster walls set off many fine stained-glass windows, including windows by Abbey Studios 1937, Sadie McLellan 1972 and Susan Laidler 1980. Pipe organ of 1912 by Ingram of Edinburgh. Attractive garden.

- Sunday: 11.00am. Bible lunch after morning service on 2nd Sunday of the month
- Open Tuesday to Friday 9.45–11.45am. Ring bell on door from Battlefield Road (0141 632 4206)

48 EASTWOOD PARISH CHURCH

5 Mansewood Road Glasgow G43 1TW

NS 558 607

Church of Scotland

Built 1863, in transitional Gothic, arranged on a cruciform plan. Designed by Charles Wilson (who died before its completion), assisted by David Thomson. Its stained-glass windows include examples by the Königliche Glasmalerei-Anstalt, München (Royal Glass-painting Establishment, Munich) and by Gordon Webster. The family church of the Maxwells of Pollok.

- Sunday: 11.15am
- Open by arrangement (0141 883 7923)

49 ST MARGARET'S
EPISCOPAL CHURCH,
NEWLANDS

353–355 Kilmarnock Road
Newlands
Glasgow
G43 2DS

A   NS 569 610

Scottish Episcopal

www.st-margarets.gn.apc.org

The church, a 'classic of the Romanesque Revival', was designed by Peter MacGregor Chalmers and built in stages between 1910 and 1935. A Romanesque-style basilica church with a double apse. The apses contain mosaics of *Christ in Glory* and the *Descent of the Holy Spirit*. The stained-glass windows include examples by Morris & Co., the St Enoch Studio and Gordon Webster and three new windows by John Clark.

- Sunday: 9.00am and 10.30am, Evensong as announced; Tuesday: 10.30am
- Open by arrangement (0141 636 1131)

50 SOUTH SHAWLANDS
CHURCH

14 Regwood Street
Glasgow
G41 3JG

A   NS 569 615

Church of Scotland

www.southshawlandschurch.org.uk

Junction with Deanston Drive, off Kilmarnock Road

Perpendicular Gothic by Miller & Black, dedicated in 1913. An unusual feature of the interior is the cantilevered gallery. Beautiful stained glass, including a window in the chancel by Douglas Hamilton 1959.

- Sunday: 11.00am all year, and 6.30pm on 2nd Sunday of the month
- Open by arrangement (0141 649 4656)

 (by arrangement)

51 SHAWLANDS UNITED REFORMED CHURCH

**111 Moss-side Road
Shawlands
Glasgow
G41 3TP**

Ⓐ NS 570 622

🚪 United Reformed Church

🌐 www.shawlands-urc.co.uk

300 metres from Shawlands Cross, on corner of Dinmont Road

The United Reformed Church in Shawlands is the successor to the first congregation of Churches of Christ founded in Glasgow in 1839. Designed by Miller & Black in 1908 in Arts and Crafts Gothic and built in red sandstone. Experience friendship, fellowship and acceptance with us; people of all ages and backgrounds are welcome.

- Sunday: 11.00am
- Open by arrangement (0141 639 9059)

52 QUEEN'S PARK BAPTIST CHURCH

**20 Balvicar Drive
Glasgow
G42 4RT**

Ⓐ NS 579 624

🚪 Baptist

🌐 www.qpbc.org

Junction of Balvicar Drive and Balvicar Street

'QP', an evangelical-charismatic church, is a changing church with growth in fellowship, preaching, ministry, outreach and worship. The church occupies two sites: services are held in the Camphill Building at 20 Balvicar Drive, and the offices are at 180 Queen's Drive. The Balvicar Drive church is a magnificent French Gothic Revival building with a soaring spire designed by William Leiper, 1876. The Camphill Building is designed in Romanesque style by McKissack & Rowan, 1887. The interiors of both buildings have been modernised and renovated.

- Sunday: 10.30am, 6.30pm and 8.00pm
- Open by arrangement (0141 423 3962)

 (Camphill)   (Queen's Drive)

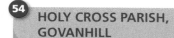

53 QUEEN'S PARK CHURCH

**170 Queen's Drive
Strathbungo
Glasgow
G42 8QZ**

A NS 579 625

⛪ Church of Scotland

🌐 www.qpp.org.uk

Junction with Albert Avenue

Nave-and-aisles Gothic church with spire, on corner site, by James Thomson 1873–5. Halls added 1879. Galleried interior with two tiers of cast-iron columns and a barrel-vaulted roof. Stained-glass window by Daniel Cottier and some exposed wall decoration. Memorial windows to Jane M. Haining. War Memorial plaques for Queen's Park West, Strathbungo, Queen's Park High and Crosshill Queen's Park Church. Alterations 2007.

- Sunday: 11.00am and 6.00pm
- Open Monday to Friday 10.00am–12.00 noon or by arrangement (0141 423 3654)

     (by arrangement)

54 HOLY CROSS PARISH, GOVANHILL

**113 Dixon Avenue
Glasgow
G42 8ER**

A NS 586 624

⛪ Roman Catholic

🌐 www.holycrossparish.org.uk

Linked with Our Lady of Consolation (55)

Junction with Belleisle Street

Romanesque-style church designed by Pugin & Pugin and opened in 1911. Rich interior with marble altar and reredos. Stained-glass windows above the sanctuary by Hardman, representing St John the Evangelist and St Margaret of Scotland, and above the gallery depicting the Exaltation of the Holy Cross, St Peter, St Andrew, St Helen and St Sylvester. Mosaic of 1961 of *Christ Triumphant* above the altar. Organ by Forster & Andrews, built 1895 for Alva Parish Church and installed 1983. Stations of the Cross by Beyeart.

- Saturday: Vigil 6.00pm; Sunday: 8.30am and 11.30am
- Open Monday to Saturday 9.00am–7.00pm (0141 423 0105)

55 OUR LADY OF CONSOLATION, GOVANHILL

Inglefield Street
Govanhill
Glasgow
G42 7DE

NS 588 630

Roman Catholic

www.holycrossparish.org.uk

Linked with Holy Cross Parish
Church (54)

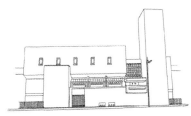

The parish of Our Lady of Consolation
was founded in 1966 and merged
with Holy Cross in 2004. The church
building, opened in 1971 and
designed by Scott, Fraser & Browning,
is typical of a construction of its
time in boxy concrete and brick. The
church is on the first floor, accessed
by lift and stairs contained within
the tall, square tower. Our Lady of
Consolation is also the Archdiocese
Youth Centre.

- Sunday: Masses 10.00am and 7.00pm
  (Diocesan Youth Mass)
- Sunday prior to Masses (0141 423
  5188)

56 ST NINIAN'S, POLLOKSHIELDS

1 Albert Drive
Pollokshields
Glasgow
G41 2PE

NS 582 632

Scottish Episcopal

www.stniniansglasgow.org.uk

The foundation stone of St Ninian's
was laid in 1872, and building
commenced to a design by David
Thomson. Completed in 1877, and
extended west in 1887. The apse is
decorated with frescoes painted
by William Hole 1901, and the
charming little sacristy designed
by H. D. Wilson, a member of the
congregation, in 1914. Good stained
glass, including windows by Heaton,
Butler & Bayne. The windows in the
chancel represent *The Gospel Story*, by
Stephen Adam.

- Sunday: Holy Communion (Said)
  8.30am and Sung Eucharist 10.15am;
  Tuesday: 6.00pm; Thursday: 10.00am
- Open by arrangement (0141 423 1247)

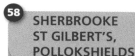

57 POLLOKSHIELDS CHURCH OF SCOTLAND

**525 Shields Road
Pollokshields
Glasgow
G41 2RF**

NS 576 634

Church of Scotland

www.pollokshieldschurch.org.uk

Junction with Albert Drive

Large Gothic church with a tall spire by Robert Baldie, 1877–8; chancel remodelled 1911–14. White marble pulpit by Peter MacGregor Chalmers. Stained glass by Stephen Adam, W. & J. J. Keir and Robert Anning Bell. Organ by Harrison & Harrison 1913. At the rear of the church are four needlework panels by Sally Moodie Harkness representing the Sun, Moon, Earth and Sea.

- Sunday: 11.00am; Wednesday: 9.45am
- Open Wednesday 10.00am–12.00 noon or by arrangement (0141 429 5425)

 (Wed 10.00–11.30am)

58 SHERBROOKE ST GILBERT'S, POLLOKSHIELDS

**240 Nithsdale Road
Pollokshields
Glasgow
G41 5AD**

NS 561 636

Church of Scotland

www.sherbrooke.org.uk

The original building by William Forsyth McGibbon was ravaged by fire in 1994, its centenary year. Now the church is marvellously restored. The interior features the work of Scottish craftsmen: stained-glass windows, inspired by the themes of creation, the Cross and rebirth, by Stained Glass Design Partnership, Kilmaurs; 3-manual pipe organ by Lammermuir Pipe Organs; pulpit, tables and font by Bill Nimmo, East Lothian.

- Sunday: 10.30am; Thursday: 10.00am
- Open by arrangement (0141 427 1968)

GLASGOW

SOUTH-WEST

59 ST JAMES'S PARISH CHURCH, POLLOK

**183 Meiklerig Crescent
Pollok
Glasgow
G53 5NA**

A NS 530 626

🏠 Church of Scotland

🌐 www.stjamespollok.co.uk

Church designed by H. E. Clifford and built in 1895 as Pollokshields Titwood Church, and moved stone by stone from its original site four miles away by Thomson, McCrae & Sanders, and rededicated in 1953. Congregation worshipped in a school hall and then in a wooden hut until the building was completed. Good stained glass. Within the sanctuary is a storytelling centre, 'The Village', which provides programmes of events for the community.

- Sunday: 11.00am
- Open by arrangement (0141 882 4984)

 (Sat 10.00am–12.00 noon)

60 ST JAMES THE GREAT, POLLOK

**20 Beltrees Road
Glasgow
G53 5TE**

A NS 525 625

🏠 Roman Catholic

Junction with Crosstobs Road

Parish established in 1949; present building by Alexander McAnally opened in 1968. The external walls are of pink Accrington brick with stone dressings and a stone façade. Inside, the walls are of cream brick and the ceiling is of cedarwood. Wrought-iron work by Thomas Bogie & Sons of Edinburgh. The circular nave can seat 544. The high altar is of various marbles.

- Saturday: 9.45am, Vigil 5.30pm; Sunday: 11.00am, daily Mass 9.45am
- Open daily 8.00–11.00am, Tuesday and Wednesday 8.00am–8.00pm (0141 882 4927)

61 **CARDONALD PARISH CHURCH**

**2155 Paisley Road West
Glasgow
G52 3PF**

⚔ NS 526 639

⛪ Church of Scotland

🌐 www.cardonaldparishchurch.com/
main

Corner of Paisley Road West and
Cardonald Place Road

Early English Gothic of Ballochmyle
red sandstone designed by Peter
MacGregor Chalmers. Chancel has
alabaster and stone pulpit by Jackson
Brown & Co. and fine workmanship
in its oak communion table, reading
desk and elders' benches. North
wall screen by Ross & Manson. Rich
and varied collection of stained-
glass windows including three-light
chancel window by J. & W. Guthrie,
series of six windows by Sadie
McLellan, Millennium window (2000)
by Roland Mitton.

- Sunday: 11.15am, Communion
  Sundays 11.15am and 6.30pm
- Open Tuesday mornings, September
  to May, 10.00–11.00am, or by
  arrangement (0141 882 6264)

62 **MOSSPARK PARISH CHURCH**

**167 Ashkirk Drive
Mosspark
Glasgow
G52 1LA**

⚔ NS 545 634

⛪ Church of Scotland

Junction with Balloch Gardens
(off Mosspark Boulevard, 1km from
M77, J1)

Congregation established 1923;
present church, designed by
Thomson, Sandilands & MacLeod,
opened in 1929. Red sandstone church
and halls with green slate roofs
in Gothic style with Art Nouveau
touches. Interior with exposed stone
and an open decorative timber roof.
White stone pulpit, communion table
and font. Pipe organ by Binns.

- Sunday: 11.00am
- Open by arrangement (0141 427 4727)

63 GOVAN AND LINTHOUSE PARISH CHURCH – GOVAN OLD BUILDING

Govan Old, St Constantine's

866 Govan Road
Govan
G51 3UU

NS 555 657
Church of Scotland
www.govanold.org.uk

Linked with Govan Cross (64),
Linthouse (65)

'The people's cathedral' sits in a churchyard dating back to Celtic times. Designed by Robert Rowand Anderson in Early English style with details based on Pluscarden Abbey near Elgin. Windows by Charles E. Kempe, Burlison & Grylls, Clayton & Bell and Shrigley & Hunt. Large collection of early medieval sculpture including hogback stones, cross shafts, cross slabs and the richly ornamented Govan Sarcophagus. Fine pipe organ originally built by Brindley & Foster.

• Monday to Friday: 10.00am
• Open Wednesday, Thursday and Saturday June to September, 1.00–4.00pm or by arrangement (0141 440 2466)

 (by arrangement)

64 GOVAN AND LINTHOUSE PARISH CHURCH – GOVAN CROSS BUILDING

New Govan Parish Church, St Mary's

Govan Cross
796 Govan Road
Govan
G51 2YL

NS 552 658
Church of Scotland

Linked with Govan Old (63),
Linthouse (65)

By Govan Underground station

This handsome Gothic church with halls was designed by Robert Baldie in 1873. Originally built as St Mary's for the United Free Church. Inside, a horseshoe-shaped gallery. Painted windows celebrate the industrial heritage of the River Clyde. The home church of the Presbytery of Glasgow.

• Sunday: 11.00am
• Open by arrangement (0141 440 2466)

 (by arrangement)
(by arrangement)

65 GOVAN AND LINTHOUSE PARISH CHURCH – LINTHOUSE BUILDING

Linthouse St Kenneth

7–9 Skipness Drive Govan G51 4RS

⚔ NS 543 658

🏠 Church of Scotland

Linked with Govan Old (63), Govan Cross (64)

The red sandstone church was originally built in 1900 as a consequence of the St Mary's United Free Church expansion into Linthouse in the late 1890s. The architect was James Miller, designer of St Enoch's, and it is the only church building designed by him which is still in use. The façade is a striking blend of classical with Arts and Crafts. A broad gable is flanked by matching square towers topped with colonnaded cupolas. The halls were added in 1953 by John S. Boyd. Embroidered church falls and table frontals from 1900–26 commissioned by the first minister and executed by Miss Webster, a member of the congregation.

- Sunday: 6.30pm
- Open by arrangement (0141 440 2466)

66 BALDERNOCK PARISH CHURCH

Baldernock Crescent Milngavie G62 6HA

⚔ NS 577 751

🏠 Church of Scotland

🌐 www.baldernockparishchurch. org.uk

1.5km (1 mile) east of A807

The religious history of the site goes back to the 13th century. The present church was built in 1795 on the site of an earlier church. The bell-tower contains a curious panel which may have come from the nearby Roman wall. The octagonal gatehouse and stone stile feature in Moffat's play *Bunty Pulls the Strings*. Interesting gravestones, including Archibald Bulloch from whom President Theodore Roosevelt and Eleanor Roosevelt descended. The church stands at the end of a lovely walk from Milngavie.

- Sunday: 11.00am
- Open Sunday 2.00–4.00pm May to August, or by arrangement (01360 620471)

67 NEW KILPATRICK PARISH CHURCH, BEARSDEN

Kirk Place
Bearsden
G61 3RT

A NS 543 723

Church of Scotland

www.nkchurch.org.uk

Off Drymen Road, A809

Building began in 1807 (James Gillespie Graham) on the site of an earlier church of 1649, and within the original settlement established by Paisley Abbey in 1232. The church was extended and the tower built in 1888 (Hugh MacLure). Very fine collection of stained glass including windows by Stephen Adam, Alfred and Gordon Webster, Norman M. Macdougall, C. E. Stewart, James Ballantine and Eilidh Keith.

- Sunday: 10.30am all year and 6.30pm September to May; Wednesday: 12.00 noon
- Open Wednesday: 1.00–3.00pm June, July and August, or by arrangement (0141 942 8827)

68 KILLERMONT PARISH CHURCH, BEARSDEN

Rannoch Drive
Bearsden
G61 2LD

A NS 556 712

Church of Scotland

www.killermontparishchurch.org.uk

Next to King George V Park

The parish was created in 1935, and the hall-church was built 1935-7, with the sanctuary opened 1957, architect Walter Ramsay. Stained glass by Gordon Webster, Sadie McLellan and Christian Shaw.

- Sunday: 10.00am all year, and 9.00am late June to mid-August; some evening services 7.00pm.
- Open by arrangement (0141 942 1413)

69 ST JAMES THE LESS, BISHOPBRIGGS

**Hilton Road
Bishopbriggs
G64 3EL**

A NS 612 712

Scottish Episcopal

⊕ www.stjamesbishopbriggs.org.uk

Built in 1980 when the congregation moved from Springburn, this church by Glasgow architects Weddell & Thomson preserves the most striking features of the 1881 Springburn building and contains many items from other Glasgow churches: stained glass by Edward Burne-Jones and Stephen Adam and part of the old high altar of Iona Abbey. Pipe organ by J. W. Walker & Sons 1964.

- Sunday: 9.00am Eucharist, 10.30am Eucharist; Thursday: 10.30am Eucharist
- Open Sunday and Thursday 10.00am–12.00 noon, or by arrangement (0141 563 5154)

70 CADDER PARISH CHURCH

**Cadder Road
Bishopbriggs
G64 3JJ**

A NS 616 723

Church of Scotland

⊕ www.cadderchurch.org.uk

A simple country church in a delightful and peaceful setting, built 1825 to designs by David Hamilton. The chancel was added in 1908 and the gallery altered 1914. Finely carved screen at the front of the gallery of Austrian oak. Very fine stained-glass windows by Steven Adam, Alfred Webster, Sadie McLellan and Crear McCartney. Pipe organ by Norman & Beard. Watch-house and cast-iron mortsafe in the graveyard.

- Sunday: 10.30am in summer
- Open by arrangement (0141 772 1363)

71 ST DAVID'S MEMORIAL PARK CHURCH, KIRKINTILLOCH

**Alexandra Street
Kirkintilloch
G66 1EA**

A NS 654 737

⛪ Church of Scotland

🌐 www.sdmp.co.uk

Off A803

The present church by Peter MacGregor Chalmers built in 1926, adjacent to the site of the original building of 1843, was dedicated as a gift of Mrs Paton Thomson in memory of her parents. In late Scottish Gothic, the church has a nave, aisles and a tower topped with a spire. Two-manual pipe organ, a significant Anneessens of 1899, rebuilt and enlarged. The existing halls were redesigned, modernised and supplemented with additional rooms in 2007.

- Sunday: 11.00am morning worship; Tuesday: 12.00 noon–12.15pm short lunchtime service
- Open by arrangement (0141 776 4989)

72 ST FLANNAN'S, KIRKINTILLOCH

**91 Hillhead Road
Kirkintilloch
G66 2HY**

A NS 663 743

⛪ Roman Catholic

Parish founded 1948. The present building, close to the Antonine Wall, was designed by William Gilmour and opened in 1970. The form of the building represents praying hands.

- Saturday: 7.00pm; Sunday: 10.00am, 12.00 noon, 6.30pm; Monday: 7.00pm
- Open by arrangement (0141 776 2310)

73 CAMPSIE PARISH CHURCH, LENNOXTOWN

**Main Street
Lennoxtown
G66 7HA**

NS 629 777

Church of Scotland

Modern timber-framed church with large entrance hall. Interesting wood carving and stained glass. Craft centre and old church with fascinating graveyard at Campsie Glen, 3.2km (2 miles).

- Sunday: 11.00am
- Open by arrangement (01360 310939)

74 ST CYPRIAN'S CHURCH, LENZIE

**Beech Road
Lenzie
G66 4HN**

NS 653 727

Scottish Episcopal

1.5km (1 mile) north of Lenzie Cross

Built in 1873 by Alexander Ross of Inverness in Gothic style with a three-stage tower at the east end and a gabled porch at the west end. The use of contrasting materials gives a colourful interior. Painting of the Last Supper on the reredos. Memorial choir screen made in local iron foundry.

- Sunday: 8.30am, 11.00am and 6.30pm (not July and August)
- Open by arrangement (0141 772 2907)

75 CAIRNS CHURCH, MILNGAVIE

**Buchanan Street
Milngavie
G62 8AW**

NS 556 748

Church of Scotland

www.cairnschurch.org.uk

The longest-serving congregation in Milngavie. Services were first held on Barloch Moor before the first building was erected in 1799. The present church was built to the design of J. B. Wilson in a late decorated Gothic style, and was opened in 1903. The red-tiled spire rises above the surrounding roofs. New halls and rooms by Page & Park, 2000, and chancel and sanctuary remodelled 2004 with the whole church enhanced by new lighting and sound systems. The church is intimate, welcoming and friendly: a partnership with history. Interior features a range of banners.

- Sunday: 10.45am and 6.30pm (summer 10.00am only)
- Open by arrangement (0141 956 4868)

76 ST PAUL'S, MILTON OF CAMPSIE

**16 Birdston Road
Milton of Campsie
G66 8BU**

NS 652 768

Roman Catholic

www.saintpaulsmilton.org.uk

Linked with St Dominic's, Torrance (77), St Patrick's, Kilsyth (91)

Worship began in 1968 in a former tartan-weaving shed alongside the present presbytery; it is now the church hall. The current church was consecrated in 1982, a single-storey building with a pyramidal roof. Inside, lots of timber gives warmth. Wooden statue of St Paul.

- Sunday: 9.30am and 4.30pm; Monday, Wednesday, Saturday: 9.00am; Thursday: 7.00pm
- Open by arrangement (01360 310355)

77 ST DOMINIC'S, TORRANCE

**School Road
Torrance
G64 4BZ**

Ａ NS 620 743

Roman Catholic

🌐 www.saintdominicstorrance.org.
uk

Linked with St Paul's, Milton of
Campsie (76), St Patrick's, Kilsyth
(91)

Prefabricated timber-framed hall of
1903 by Speirs, Dick & Smith. Clad
in harled brick in 1959, it became
the Catholic church in 1979. Simple
interior enlivened by a relief of the
Last Supper round the base of the
altar.

- Saturday: Vigil 6.30pm; Sunday:
  11.00am; Tuesday and Friday: 9.00am
- Open by arrangement (01360 310355)

78 NEW MONKLAND PARISH CHURCH, AIRDRIE

**Condorrat Road, Glenmavis
Airdrie
ML6 0NS**

Ａ NS 753 678

Church of Scotland

🌐 www.new-monkland-church.
freeserve.co.uk/pages/index.htm

Linked with Greengairs Parish
Church (89)

A fine old Scots plain kirk which
hides an attractive interior, by
Andrew Bell of Airdrie 1776. It holds a
commanding position at the highest
point in the village, and incorporates
the bell-tower of an earlier church
(1698) which housed a cell for minor
offenders. The old church was
replaced when it suffered so badly
from overcrowding that youthful
members of the congregation
colonised the exposed joists to roost!
The apse was added in 1904 by John
Arthur. Extensive restoration 1997,
internal alterations 2007. Simple
watch-house by the cemetery.

- Sunday: 10.00am
- Open by arrangement (01236 763554)

79 FLOWERHILL PARISH CHURCH, AIRDRIE

**Hallcraig Street
Airdrie
ML6 6AW**

⋏ NS 764 655

🏠 Church of Scotland

🌐 www.flowerhillparishchurch.co.uk

Opened in 1875, architect Matthew Forsyth of Airdrie, who designed the church, campanile, manse and hall in Italianate style. Major refurbishment 2002–3. Six stained-glass windows by Stephen Adam, James Ballantine, J. T. Stewart and J. S. Melville. Pipe organ 1886, by Harrison & Harrison.

- Sunday: 11.00am all year and 6.30pm September to June
- Open by arrangement (01236 754430)

80 ST MARGARET'S, AIRDRIE

**96 Hallcraig Street
Airdrie
ML6 6AW**

⋏ NS 765 656

🏠 Roman Catholic

🌐 www.stmargaretsairdrie.org.uk

Parish founded in 1836; this neoclassical church by Wilkie & Gray, 1839, has a square tower and spire rising above the pedimented front. The simple exterior belies the magnificent interior with its classical reredos with an elaborate cornice behind the main altar flanked by two side altars in marble. Before it was built, adherents had to travel to Glasgow for services, many on foot.

- Saturday: Vigil 5.00pm; Sunday: 10.00am, 12.00 noon and 4.00pm
- Open 8.30–10.45am weekdays; 8.30am–1.30pm Sunday (01236 763370)

81 BONKLE CHURCH

**Church Road
Bonkle
ML2 9QG**

⚓ NS 837 570
⛪ Church of Scotland
🌐 www.coltness-memorial.org.uk

Linked with Coltness Memorial
Church, Newmains (96)

Simple Gothic-style church of 1878
built in honey-coloured sandstone.
Traditional reformed-tradition
interior with the pulpit on the south
wall and a balcony round the other
three sides. Three large stained-glass
windows are in the wall above the
pulpit.

- Sunday: 12.00 noon, 6.30pm (evening
  service alternates with Coltness
  Memorial Church)
- Open by arrangement (01698 344001)
  (Coltness Memorial Church Office,
  Thursday mornings only)

82 CORPUS CHRISTI,
CALDERBANK

**Calderbank
ML6 9TA**

⚓ NS 768 630
⛪ Roman Catholic
🌐 www.corpuschristicalderbank.
co.uk

In the middle of Calderbank village

The parish was founded in 1948, and
the church was opened in 1952. It
has undergone several renovations
inside to accommodate liturgical
changes. Stained-glass window of the
sacraments 1985, designed by Shona
McInnes. New church furnishings by
J. McNally, made by a local craftsman.

- Saturday: 8.45am and Vigil 6.00pm;
  Sunday: 9.00am, 11.00am; weekdays:
  10.00am
- Open 8.00am–8.00pm; if main door
  closed, use right-hand side door
  (01236 763670)

83 ST FRANCIS XAVIER CHURCH, CARFIN

Carfin Lourdes Grotto

**Taylor Avenue
Carfin
ML1 5AJ**

NS 776 588

Roman Catholic

www.carfin.org.uk

Off Newarthill Road, B7066

The parish was founded in 1862; the present church dates from 1973, the hall from 2008. The church grounds contain the Carfin Lourdes grotto, founded in the 1920s, which is open throughout the year, with public services from May to mid-October on Sundays at 3.00pm. Glass chapel in memory of Lockerbie tragedy dedicated to Our Lady, Maid of the Seas is open 10.00am–8.00pm Easter to October.

- Saturday: Vigil 5.30pm; Sunday: 9.00am, 12.00 noon; weekdays: 10.00am; May to October weekdays: 1.00pm
- Open in summer 9.00am–8.00pm, winter 9.00am–4.00pm (01698 263308)

    (Pilgrimage Centre)

84 ST ALOYSIUS, CHAPELHALL

**192 Main Street
Chapelhall
ML6 8SF**

NS 783 626

Roman Catholic

Opened in 1894, built to a design by Pugin & Pugin. Sanctuary completely renewed 1941–52. Marble reredos with gold mosaic panels depicting scenes from the life of St Aloysius. Stained glass installed in rose window 1984 by Shona McInnes of Orkney, who also designed the remaining four windows in the sanctuary, installed 1994 to celebrate the church centenary. Beautiful gardens behind the church, with excellent presbytery house designed by McInally.

- Saturday: Vigil 6.30pm; Sunday: 10.00am, 12.00 noon and 5.30pm
- Open daily 9.00am–7.30pm (01236 763190)

85 ## NEW ST ANDREW'S PARISH CHURCH, COATBRIDGE

**Church Street
Coatbridge
ML5 3EB**

Λ NS 733 653

🏠 Church of Scotland

🌐 www.saintandrewscoatbridge.org

This red sandstone Gothic Revival church with steeple and clock tower, by Scott, Stephen & Gale, was opened in 1839 for the benefit of the workers of Wm Baird & Co., Ironmasters, and their families. It occupies a commanding site with a large graveyard just a short walk uphill from the town centre. In 1993, it became St Andrew's following a union with nearby Dunbeth and Maxwell churches. In October 2008, it united with Clifton Church and became New St Andrew's Parish Church. Very fine organ by Willis, 1870, renovated in 1937 with additional stops. Stained glass by Alfred Webster, 1912, in the entrance vestibule.

- Sunday: 11.00am; 6.00pm on 3rd Sunday of the month except July and August
- Open by arrangement (01236 431385)

86 ## ST PATRICK'S, COATBRIDGE

**Main Street
Coatbridge
ML5 3HB**

Λ NS 733 651

🏠 Roman Catholic

🌐 www.stpatricks-online.com

Built for the many Irish labourers fleeing the potato famine, and for dispossessed Highlanders. Designed by Pugin & Pugin 1896, in elegant Gothic with a finely composed gable frontage. Splendid original marble altar with Gothic reredos.

- Saturday: Vigil 6.00pm; Sunday: 10.00am, 12.00 noon and 6.00pm; weekdays 10.00am
- Open 10.00am–4.30pm (01236 606808)

87

CUMBERNAULD OLD PARISH CHURCH

**19–21 Baronhill
The Village
Cumbernauld
G67 2SD**

NS 765 760

Church of Scotland

www.cumbernauldold.org.uk

This ancient building owes its foundations to an early chapel built by the Comyn family at the end of the 12th or beginning of the 13th century. The chapel fell into disuse after the Reformation but was rebuilt in 1650 and greatly extended in 1659. The wallheads were raised and galleries inserted at the end of the 18th century.

- Sunday: 10.15am (11.00am on 1st Sunday of March, June, September and December)
- Open by arrangement (01236 721912)

88

ST LUCY'S, CUMBERNAULD

**9 Pine Crescent
Abronhill
Cumbernauld
G67 3NG**

NS 785 760

Roman Catholic

www.stlucys.co.uk

The parish was founded in 1973 to serve the satellite housing estate of Abronhill, and the church building opened in 1976. The church is a simple box, but with an interior made warm and welcoming with wooden pews and light from clerestory windows. There has been considerable upgrading in recent years and an expansion of the community use of the hall.

- Saturday: Vigil 6.30pm; Sunday: 11am and 6pm; weekdays: 9.30am
- Open daily 8.30am–10.30pm (01236 724894)

NORTH LANARKSHIRE

89

GREENGAIRS PARISH CHURCH

New Monkland linked with Greengairs

Greengairs Road
Greengairs
ML6 7TE

🜊 NS 783 705

⛪ Church of Scotland

🌐 www.greengairs-church.freeserve.co.uk

Linked with New Monkland Parish Church, Airdrie (78)

On B803 at west end of village

Greengairs is a village of North Lanarkshire which developed in the 19th century in association with coal mining and quarrying. The parish church was erected in the 1870s in a simple Gothic Revival style.

- Sunday: 11.15am
- Open by arrangement (01236 763554)

 90

BURNS AND OLD PARISH CHURCH, KILSYTH

Backbrae Street
Kilsyth
G65 0NF

🜊 NS 716 778

⛪ Church of Scotland

🌐 www.boldchurch.org.uk

Gothic-style stone-built church with battlemented tower built in 1816 and refurbished in 1932, architect Mr Shepherd. The tower, clock and bell were gifted by Sir Charles Edmonstone of Duntreath. Pipe organ by Conacher.

- Sunday: 11.00am, and 6.30pm on 2nd Sunday of the month October to June
- Open occasional Saturday mornings, otherwise by arrangement (01236 823241)

91 ST PATRICK'S, KILSYTH

**30 Low Craigends
Kilsyth
G65 0PF**

NS 720 777

Roman Catholic

www.saintpatrickskilsyth.org.uk

Linked with St Paul's, Milton of Campsie (76), St Dominic's, Torrance (77)

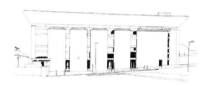

The first church of 1866 was replaced in 1965 by the present modern church by Gillespie, Kidd & Coia. A large-scale brick box surmounted by a clerestory and unusual roof. Large, spacious interior with light entering by the clerestory windows and carefully placed roof lights. The layout conforms to the requirements of the Second Vatican Council. One of only four Gillespie, Kidd & Coia churches with all its original features intact. Fully restored 2000.

- Saturday: Vigil 6.00pm; Sunday: 9.30am and 12.00 noon; weekdays: 10.00am
- Open by arrangement (01236 822136)

92 ST MARY'S PARISH CHURCH, MOTHERWELL

**76 Avon Street
Motherwell
ML1 3AB**

NS 750 566

Church of Scotland

St Mary's was designed in 1914 by Peter MacGregor Chalmers in Romanesque style. The cruciform church was built of honey-coloured Auchenheath sandstone. Three stained-glass windows, 1923, commemorate the founding minister; three, by Gordon Webster, 1968, depict Christ the Carpenter and four saints, and tell the story of the church. Allen Q–345 organ, 2007.

- Sunday: 11.00am
- Open by arrangement (01698 268554)

93 **DALZIEL ST ANDREW'S PARISH CHURCH, MOTHERWELL**

The Kirk at the Cross

**43–47 Merry Street
The Cross
Motherwell
ML1 1JJ**

Ⓐ NS 752 571

🏛 Church of Scotland

Union of the former Dalziel and St Andrew's Church of Scotland congregations in 1996. The parish of Dalziel has a history stretching back to the 12th century, while St Andrew's was a daughter church of Dalziel. Erected in 1874, the building houses an organ by the German firm of Walcker dated 1900, recently restored. Worship is a sensitive mixture of traditional and modern with a warm welcome for all ages.

- Sunday: 11.00am and 6.30pm September to June, 10.30am only July and August
- Open by arrangement (01698 263414)

94 ST LUKE'S, MOTHERWELL

**Davaar Drive
Forgewood
Motherwell
ML1 3TW**

Ⓐ NS 746 589

🏛 Roman Catholic

🌐 www.stlukesmotherwell.org.uk

St Luke's Parish was established in 1954 and the church was built in 1955. A recently renovated church whose intimate setting serves well the Liturgy of the Second Vatican Council. His Eminence Cardinal Thomas Winning, RIP, was parish priest from 1966 to 1970.

- Saturday: 9.30am, 5.15pm; Sunday: 10.30am, 5.15pm; weekdays: 9.30am
- Open by arrangement (01698 230402)

95 ST BRENDAN'S, MOTHERWELL

**51 Barons Road
Motherwell
ML1 2NB**

NS 769 549

Roman Catholic

St Brendan's was founded as a parish in 1965, and the present church was built in 1968 and renovated in 1994. A modern and comfortable church. Presbytery, hall and school are next to the church.

- Saturday: Vigil 6.00pm; Sunday: 11.00am; weekdays: 9.30am
- Open by arrangement (01698 264448)

96 COLTNESS MEMORIAL CHURCH, NEWMAINS

**Kirkgate
Newmains
ML2 9BD**

NS 819 558

Church of Scotland

www.coltness-memorial.org.uk

Linked with Bonkle Church (81)

Norman-Gothic, 1878, designed by W. Wallace of London. Notable for the striking and intricate polychrome brickwork of the interior. Pulpit and font in Caen stone with pillars of dark serpentine marble. Linen-fold oak panelling in the chancel. Good collection of stained glass, including windows by Stephen Adam. Two-manual organ, 1878, by Thomas Lewis & Son.

- Sunday: 10.30am, 6.30pm (evening service alternates with Bonkle Church)
- Open usually 9.00am–5.00pm (01698 344001; church office, Thursday mornings only)

 (by arrangement)

NORTH LANARKSHIRE

97 ST BRIGID'S, NEWMAINS

**5 Westwood Road
Newmains
ML2 9DA**

⚐ NS 822 560

⛪ Roman Catholic

🌐 www.stbrigid.org.uk

A well-used parish church and flourishing parish centre standing in its own grounds. The original church of 1871 is now the parish centre; the present church was built in 1933. Light airy interior is lit by clerestory windows over an open arcade.

- Saturday: 10.00am, Vigil 5.30pm; Sunday: 9.30am and 12.00 noon; weekdays: 9.30am
- Open daily 9.00am–5.00pm (01698 297037)

98 OVERTOWN PARISH CHURCH

**Main Street
Overtown
ML2 0QP**

⚐ NS 801 527

⛪ Church of Scotland

Village church described in Groome's Gazetteer as 'built in 1874–5 at a cost of over £2,000 ... an early English edifice, with a bold square tower 80 feet high, and 600 sittings'. New halls built alongside behind the war memorial. Near picturesque Clyde Valley, Strathclyde Country Park and many other places of interest.

- Sunday: 11.00am, evening service 6.30pm last Sunday in February, June and October
- Open by arrangement (01698 372330)

99 ST PATRICK, SHOTTS

**84 Station Road
Shotts
ML7 4BJ**

NS 876 599

Roman Catholic

www.saintpatrick.org.uk

The church, designed by P. P. Pugin, is a classic example of his work. White Carrara marble altar and reredos added 1930s. Stained glass depicts Crucifixion and scenes of the local pits and iron works, as well as St Barbara (patron saint of miners), St Joseph, St Cecilia, St John Ogilvie and the *Baptism of the Lord*. Stations of the Cross are from Germany. The church has been adapted to changing liturgical practice while retaining its original character and quality.

- Saturday: 9.30am, Vigil 6.30pm; Sunday: 10.45am, Sung Mass with Choir 6.00pm; weekdays: 10.00am
- Open Monday to Thursday 9.00am–1.00pm, Friday 9.00am–6.00pm (01501 821838)

100 STEPPS PARISH CHURCH

**17 Whitehill Avenue
Stepps
G33 6BL**

NS 657 686

Church of Scotland

www.steppsparishchurch.org.uk

Fine example of the neo-Gothic style favoured by ecclesiastical architect Peter MacGregor Chalmers, 1900. Designed to reflect scale and simplicity of a village church. Built of red Ballochmyle sandstone in the form of a cross. Interesting stained glass including works by Stephen Adam, 1900. Pipe organ, Joseph Brook 1884, rebuilt James MacKenzie 1976.

- Sunday: 11.00am mid-August to mid-June, 9.30am and 11.00am mid-June to mid-August
- Open by arrangement with the minister, Rev. Neil Buchanan (0141 779 5746)

101 ST IGNATIUS OF LOYOLA, WISHAW

74 Young Street
Wishaw
ML2 8HS

NS 799 551

Roman Catholic

www.saintignatiuswishaw.org.uk/index.html

Designed by George Goldie and opened in 1865, enlarged by Bruce & Hay 1883. Built in basilica form with two aisles and a bell-tower which is the most prominent landmark in Wishaw. The tower houses a bell (tone E) which is rung every day at 12.00 noon and 6.00pm for the Angelus prayer and also 30 minutes before the main Sunday service and during weekday services. Stained-glass windows based on paintings by Jessie McGeechan of Coatbridge.

- Saturday: 10.00am, Vigil 5.30pm; Sunday: 10.15am, 12.00 noon, 6.00pm; weekdays: 9.30am
- Open Sunday 9.30am–1.30pm and 5.30–7.30pm; Monday to Friday 8.30am–1.30pm (Thursday 4.30pm); Saturday 9.00am–12.00 noon and 5.00–7.00pm (01698 372058)

102 AUCHENGRAY CHURCH

Auchengray
ML11 8LN

NS 995 540

Church of Scotland

Linked with Tarbrax Church (149)

4.5km (3 miles) west of A70

This church of 1863 by F. T. Pilkington with characteristic stone carving and a fine rose window is described as an architectural gem. The building and grounds are undergoing a programme of restoration and upgrading to ensure an ongoing welcome at the heart of the community.

- Sunday: 6.30pm September to June, usually on 1st Sunday of the month; no services July and August
- Open by arrangement (01501 785413)

103 BIGGAR KIRK

Kirkstyle
Biggar
ML12 6DA

NT 040 379

Church of Scotland

Linked with Culter Parish Church (115), Black Mount Parish Church (117), Libberton and Quothquan Parish Church (138)

Rebuilt 1546, the last collegiate church to be founded in Scotland before the Reformation. A cruciform building with fine stained glass, including work by William Wilson and Crear McCartney. In the kirkyard are memorials to the forebears of William Ewart Gladstone and also Thomas Blackwood Murray, the Scottish motor pioneer of 'Albion'.

- Sunday: 11.00am; also 9.30am June, July and August
- Open daily June, July and August 10.00am–4.00pm, or key from Gillespie Centre across the street (01899 220227)

104 OUR LADY AND ST JOHN, BLACKWOOD

Carlisle Road
Blackwood
ML11 9RZ

NS 790 439

Roman Catholic

www.ourladyandstjohns blackwood.co.uk

North end of Blackwood, by M74

Stone building in Gothic style by Robert Ingram. The church was built in 1880 as a private chapel, with the parish formed in 1896. The grounds for the church were donated by the Hope-Vere family. Sanctuary extended in 1881 to accommodate the altar donated by Mrs Lancaster. Stained-glass windows were also added at this time. The first two parish priests were Benedictines from Ampleforth.

- Saturday: 6.00pm; Sunday: 10.00am and 6.00pm
- Open by arrangement (01555 893459)

SOUTH LANARKSHIRE

105 BOTHWELL PARISH CHURCH

Main Street
Bothwell
G71 8EX

⚐ NS 705 586

🏛 Church of Scotland

🌐 www.bothwellparishchurch.org

In centre of Bothwell, off A725

Scotland's oldest collegiate church still in use for worship, dedicated to St Bride, occupying the site of a former 6th-century church. Medieval choir. Nave and tower 1833, David Hamilton, altered 1933. Monuments to the Earls of Douglas and the Duke of Hamilton. Stained glass by Gordon Webster, Douglas Strachan and Sir Edward Burne-Jones. Fascinating tales of an outstanding royal wedding and link with Bothwell Castle. Graveyard.

- Sunday: 10.30am
- Open daily June to end August, 10.00am–12.30pm and 2.00–4.00pm (01698 853189)

106 ST BRIDE'S, BOTHWELL

Fallside Road
Bothwell
G71 8BA

⚐ NS 706 550

🏛 Roman Catholic

🌐 www.rcdom.org.uk/parishes_ stbrides_bothwell.htm

This impressive and striking building was opened in 1973. The concrete block walls are rendered externally to harmonise with the surrounding buildings. The red knotty pine ceiling and quarry tile floor bring warmth to the interior, and coloured blocks of glass have been used to contrast with the white walls. Superb pipe organ, striking modern statue of Mary, and a modern sculpture of the Last Supper. Convent of Poor Clares next door to the church can also be visited.

- Saturday: Vigil 5.30pm; Sunday: 10.00am, 12.00 noon and 6.00pm; Advent and Lent Prayer Service at 5.15pm; weekdays: 9.30am
- Open Tuesday and Wednesday 10.00am–8.00pm or by arrangement (01698 852710)

107 CAMBUSLANG OLD PARISH CHURCH

3 Cairns Road, Kirkhill Cambuslang G72 8PX

⚐ NS 646 600

⛪ Church of Scotland

🌐 www.cambuslang-old-parish-church.com

Near Greenlees Road, B759

St Cadoc is believed to have had a holy site here c. AD 550, and early buildings have been recorded from the 12th century. The present building is by David Cousin 1841 and the chancel is by Peter MacGregor Chalmers 1922. Steeple with clock and bell. Stained glass and tapestries by Sadie McLellan 1957. Millennium wall-hanging in vestibule 2001. Heraldic shields of heritors decorate the ceiling. Interesting gravestones in churchyard, including one to Rev. William McCulloch, minister at Scotland's largest-ever revival, 'The Cambuslang Wark' in 1742.

- Sunday: September to June 11.00am and 6.30pm, July and August 9.30am and 11.00am
- Open by arrangement (0141 641 3261)

108 ST CUTHBERT'S, CAMBUSLANG

3 Brownside Road Cambuslang G72 8NL

⚐ NS 643 604

⛪ Scottish Episcopal

Linked with St Andrew's, Uddingston (150)

Towards the end of the 19th century, Cambuslang became an increasingly residential area and the need arose for an Episcopal church. In 1899, Bishop W. T. Harrison opened a hall on Bushley Hill for worship dedicated to St Cuthbert. Subsequently, the Duke of Hamilton offered land, and the present church was dedicated in 1909, architect W. D. Walton of Glasgow.

- Sunday: 9.30am (Sung Eucharist); Wednesday: 10.00am (Said Eucharist)
- Open every morning during term-time (0141 641 1173)

109 ST BRIDE'S, CAMBUSLANG

21 Greenlees Road Cambuslang G72 8JB

Å NS 643 604

Roman Catholic

www.saintbrides.com

Opposite police station

The church, which opened in 1900, was originally intended to be the church hall. Crucifixion window, an example of the early work of stained-glass artist Gordon M. Webster, and another free-standing window, the *Calling of the Apostles*, also by Webster. Icons of St Joseph, St Bride and Christ in Glory by icon-painter Sr Petra Clare.

- Saturday: Vigil 5.30pm; Sunday: 10.00am, 12.00 noon, 3.30pm and 6.00pm
- Open 7.00am–9.00pm every day (0141 641 3053)

110 ST ANDREW'S PARISH CHURCH, CARLUKE

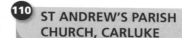

Mount Stewart Street Carluke ML8 5EB

Å NS 843 508

Church of Scotland

The original church was replaced by the present building in 1799 to designs by Henry Bell (of the steamship *Comet* fame). The tower of the old church has been retained as a monument in its original site in the old graveyard at the bottom of the town. Within the church are an organ made by H. Willis & Sons and installed in 1903, stained-glass windows including one made by Gordon McWhirter Webster 1932 and a pulpit fall and companion communion-table runner by Marilyn E. W. McGregor DA 1999. Memorial garden, 'Garden of Hope' 2001.

- Sunday: 11.00am
- Open by arrangement (01555 773595)

111 ST ATHANASIUS, CARLUKE

21 Mount Stewart Street
Carluke
ML8 5EB

🅰 NS 844 508

🛐 Roman Catholic

🌐 www.stathanasius.co.uk

A church was first erected in 1857, but a larger building was required by the 1980s when the building was extended as far as the grounds allowed. The marriage of old and new buildings in 1984 has given a modern and attractive church while still retaining much of the original character. The architects were Cullen, Lochhead & Brown.

- Saturday: Vigil 6.00pm; Sunday: 9.00am, 11.15am and 5.30pm; weekdays: 10.00am
- Open 9.00am–4.00pm daily (01555 771250)

    (by arrangement)

112 CAIRNGRYFFE KIRK, CARMICHAEL

Carmichael
ML12 6PQ

🅰 NS 923 384

🛐 Church of Scotland

🌐 www.cairngryffekirk.org.uk

Linked with Symington Kirk (148)

Carmichael Crossroads

Known as 'The Little Cathedral of the Upper Ward', due to the quality of the decoration, this church was built 1750 and extensively remodelled 1904 by Sir Robert Lorimer. The staircase to the gallery and several headstones were brought from the site of the 12th-century church a mile away. Magnificent stained-glass window 1904. Other glass by Crear McCartney. Many memorials to the Carmichael family and clan.

- Sunday: 9.30am or 11.00am as indicated on notice-board
- Open by arrangement (01899 308397)

113 **CARNWATH PARISH CHURCH**

St Mary's

Carnwath
ML11 8JX

⚔ NS 976 465

 Church of Scotland

West end of Carnwath on A70

St Mary's is the third building to have been constructed on the site. Built 1864–7, architect David Bryce. Seating capacity over 1,000. Roof is modelled on that of Parliament Hall in Edinburgh. Long wall pulpit.

- Sunday: 12.00 noon September to June, 11.00am July and August
- Open by arrangement. As the church is at times undergoing repairs, please phone before visiting (01355 840312).

B (church) **A** (St Mary's Aisle)

114 **COALBURN PARISH CHURCH**

25/1 Bellfield Road
Coalburn
ML11 0LA

⚔ NS 813 345

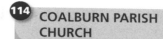 Church of Scotland

Built as a mission station 1893, becoming a fully sanctioned charge 1895. Totally destroyed by fire 1918 and rebuilt 1922. Church renovated and reordered 2001 to become all-purpose. Six ministers have served during the 110 years.

- Sunday: 12.00 noon
- Open by arrangement (01555 892425)

115 CULTER PARISH CHURCH, COULTER

**Coulter
ML12 6PZ**

NT 027 342

Church of Scotland

Linked with Biggar Kirk (103), Black Mount Parish Church (117), Libberton and Quothquan Parish Church (138)

200 metres off Birthwood Road

Appropriated by Kelso Abbey in 1170, the church is dedicated to St Michael. Rebuilt about 1810, made shorter and wider. The interior was recast 1910, with two of the galleries removed, leaving only the west one. Refurnished 1938. Ornamental gates. Chancel burial ground for Culter Allers and Culter Mains. Bertram (of Nisbet) burial aisle next to vestry.

- Sunday: 9.30am, 10.45am and 12.00 noon on a quarterly rotation with Black Mount and Libberton and Quothquan
- Open by arrangement (01899 220625)

116 DALSERF PARISH CHURCH

**Kirk Road
Dalserf
ML9 3BL**

NS 800 507

Church of Scotland

www.dalserf.org.uk

Off A72 between Garrion Bridge and Rosebank

Built 1655, centre transept added 1892. Oblong building with pulpit on long side. Outside stairs to three galleries. Belfry with elegantly slender posts. Two large memorial windows on either side of pulpit by Douglas Hogg. The graveyard contains a pre-Norman hogback stone and an outstanding Covenanting memorial. Also memorial of 1753 to Rev. John MacMillan, first minister and principal founder of the Reformed Presbyterian Church.

- Sunday: 12.00 noon September to June, 10.30am July and August
- Open Saturday from mid-May to end August 12.00 noon–4.00pm or by arrangement (01698 882195)

 (by arrangement)

SOUTH LANARKSHIRE

117 BLACK MOUNT PARISH CHURCH, DOLPHINTON

**Dolphinton
EH46 7HH**

NT 101 464

Church of Scotland

Linked with Biggar Kirk (103),
Culter Parish Church (113),
Libberton and Quothquan Parish
Church (138)

Just off A702 at Dolphinton

Originally a parsonage in the 13th
century, it appears to have always
occupied the same site, undergoing
a complete rebuild in 1789, with late
19th-century additions. A typical
T-plan church, built so the preacher
has the light behind him and the
congregation can hear him. The bell
dates from c. 1800.

- Sunday: 9.30am, 10.45am and
  12.00 noon on a quarterly rotation
  with Culter and Libberton and
  Quothquan
- Open by arrangement (01899 220625)

118 ST BRIDE'S, DOUGLAS

Douglas Parish Church

**Braehead
Douglas
ML11 0PT**

NS 835 310

Church of Scotland

www.douglasvalleychurch.org

Linked with Douglas Water and
Rigside Church (140)

Centre of Douglas, on A70

St Bride's was built 1781–2 to replace
the nearby medieval building which
had become ruinous (the refurbished
chancel and clock-tower still stand).
The church was substantially altered
in 1868 and 1878. The side drums
and pipe banner of the Cameronian
Regiment are kept in the church,
and the raising of the regiment
is commemorated on the second
Sunday of May.

- Sunday: 10.00am
- Open by arrangement (01555 850000)

  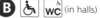 (in halls)
 (Community Centre)

119 DRUMCLOG MEMORIAL KIRK

Drumclog
ML10 6QG

⚲ NS 640 389

⛪ Church of Scotland

🌐 www.avendale-drumclog.com

Linked with Avendale Old Parish Church, Strathaven (144)

A71, 8km (5 miles) west on Darvel Road

Replacing a corrugated-iron church of 1901, the present stone church was designed by J. McLellan Fairley and opened in 1912. A solid Gothic-style church with a square tower topped with an octagonal spire clad in copper. Named Drumclog Memorial Kirk in remembrance of the Battle of Drumclog fought in 1679 when the Covenanters defeated Government troops.

- Sunday: 9.30am
- Open by arrangement (01357 521939)

120 ST BRIDE'S, EAST KILBRIDE

Whitemoss Avenue
East Kilbride
G74 1NN

⚲ NS 641 544

⛪ Roman Catholic

Linked with St Mary's, Larkhall (135)

Built 1963–4 by Gillespie, Kidd & Coia to a radical modernist design. The original 46m (150ft) campanile had to be demolished in 1966 due to the deterioration of the brickwork. This is one of the busiest churches in South Lanarkshire, with a congregation of over 8,000.

- Saturday: 10.00am and 6.00pm; Sunday: 9.00am, 10.30am, 12.00 noon and 6.00pm; weekdays: 10.00am and 1.00pm
- Open by arrangement (01355 220005)

121 GLASFORD PARISH CHURCH

**Jackson Street
Glassford
ML10 6TQ**

NS 726 470

Church of Scotland

Linked with East Parish Church, Strathaven (145)

Built 1820. Memorial stained-glass windows to Rev. Gavin Lang, grandfather of Cosmo Lang, Archbishop of Canterbury. Ruins of 1633 church and Covenanter's stone.

- Sunday: 10.00am
- Open by arrangement (01357 521138)

122 HAMILTON OLD PARISH CHURCH

**Strathmore Road
Hamilton
ML3 6AQ**

NS 723 555

Church of Scotland

In centre of town

A Georgian gem. The only church designed and built by William Adam, 1734. Samples from the roof timbers found to be full of lead shot; Adam used wood from an old man-of-war! Chancel furnishings include embroidery by Hannah Frew Paterson. Exceptionally detailed engraved-glass windows by Anita Pate depict the history of the church back to the 6th century. Memorial stained-glass window of African animals to John Stevenson Hamilton, founder of Kruger National Park. Eleventh-century Netherton Cross and Covenanting memorials in graveyard.

- Sunday: 10.45am
- Open Monday to Friday, 10.30am–3.30pm, or by arrangement (01698 281905)

123 HAMILTON WEST PARISH CHURCH

Peacock Cross
Burnbank Road
Hamilton
ML3 9AA

⚲ NS 712 558

🏛 Church of Scotland

The church was originally founded in 1874 as the 'Burnbank Mission Station' of St John's Free Church. Having been raised to full status in 1875, the church was rebuilt 1880, architect John Hutchison, whose design exhibits many features in the 13th-century Gothic style. The interior has one of the best examples in Scotland of a wooden hammerbeam roof. The organ by Hill & Son of London, 1902, is still in use today. The exterior is floodlit, highlighting the stonework which was restored in 1988.

- Sunday: 10.45am, except July 10.00am
- Open by arrangement (01698 284670)

124 ST JOHN'S CHURCH, HAMILTON

Top Cross
Duke Street
Hamilton
ML3 7DT

⚲ NS 724 553

🏛 Church of Scotland

🌐 www.stjohnshamilton.org.uk

Opposite Marks & Spencer

Idiosyncratic classical building (originally a chapel of ease) 1835. The interior was renovated in 1971 by Cullen, Lochhead & Brown, incorporating the former St John's Grammar School of 1836 and the Centenary Hall of 1934. Refurbished and extended 2000 (Cullen, Lochhead & Brown). Two works in stained glass by Susan Bradbury feature in the St John's Centre: in the chapel (*Wings*) and in the coffee room (*Giving and Receiving*).

- Sunday: 10.45am and 6.30pm (summer 10.00am and 9.00pm)
- St John's Chapel and Centre open Monday to Saturday 10.00am–4.00pm (01698 286868)

 (St John's Centre)

125 GILMOUR AND WHITEHILL PARISH CHURCH, HAMILTON

Burnbank UP Church, Burnbank UF Church, Gilmour Memorial Church

**Burnbank Centre
Burnbank
Hamilton
ML3 0NA**

A NS 704 562

Church of Scotland

Gothic hall-church with tower, built 1882–4 by Duncan McNaughtan, originally as Burnbank UP Church. Reformed church layout of central pulpit, two aisles and gallery. Several embroidered hangings. Halls added 1970s.

- Sunday: 10.30am
- Coffee lounge open 10.00am–12.00 noon, Monday to Friday (01698 284201)

126 HILLHOUSE PARISH CHURCH, HAMILTON

**Clarkwell Road
Hamilton
ML3 9TQ**

A NS 696 554

Church of Scotland

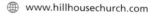 www.hillhousechurch.com

Established 1955, the church has warmly welcomed many visitors from this country and abroad during its relatively short history. Sanctuary enhanced by stained glass designed by children from local primary schools. We are a lively, go-ahead church, who believe in challenging people with the Gospel of Christ in a way that is relevant today. We promise you one thing: whatever your age, you won't be bored in Hillhouse.

- Sunday: 10.45am all year, and 7.00pm September to April
- Open by arrangement (01698 829615)

   (by arrangement)

127 CADZOW PARISH CHURCH, HAMILTON

Woodside Walk
Hamilton
ML3 7HY

 NS 723 550

 Church of Scotland

This Gothic-style church, designed by R. A. Bryden, was opened 1877 for coal miners and their families. Halls designed by Cullen, Lochhead & Brown added 1925 and 1961. Pipe organ by Forster & Andrew of Hull installed 1889. Communion table, chairs and eagle lectern are by Thomas Wilson of Glasgow. Stained-glass windows by Stephen Adam, Douglas Hamilton, John Blyth and Sadie McLellan.

- Sunday: 9.30am and 10.45am June to August; 10.45am September to May
- Open by arrangement (01698 425512)

128 ST MARY THE VIRGIN, HAMILTON

Auchingramont Road
Hamilton
ML3 6JT

 NS 721 567

 Scottish Episcopal

 www.stmarysepiscopalhamilton. co.uk

The building, designed by John Henderson, was opened for worship in 1847 and is Early English in style. Chancel ceiling panels were painted by Mabel Royds (1874–1941). There are fine stained-glass commemorative windows with several memorials in marble and stone reflecting the links with the town's military history. Organ, Forster & Andrews 1890.

- Sunday: 8.30am and 10.00am, 1st and 3rd Sunday 6.00pm; Wednesday: 10.00am
- Open by arrangement (01698 429895)

SOUTH LANARKSHIRE

SOUTH LANARKSHIRE

 129 ST MARY'S CHURCH, HAMILTON

**120 Cadzow Street
Hamilton
ML3 6HP**

NS 720 557

Roman Catholic

www.rcdom.org.uk/parishes_
stmarys_hamilton.htm

Built in 1846 in Early English style,
this is the second-oldest Catholic
church in Lanarkshire after St
Margaret's, Airdrie. St Mary's is
a much-loved building with the
parishioners. The beautiful stained
glass and woodwork provide a
tranquil setting for the celebration of
the Church's liturgy.

* Saturday: Vigil 6.00pm; Sunday:
  10.00am, 11.30am, 6.00pm; weekdays:
  10.00am
* Open weekdays 9.30am–2.00pm
  (01698 423552)

130 KIRKMUIRHILL PARISH CHURCH

**Carlisle Road
Kirkmuirhill
ML11 9RB**

NS 799 429

Church of Scotland

www.kirkmuirhillchurch.co.uk

Built in 1868 by the United
Presyterian Church, architect Robert
Baldie. Early English Gothic Revival
style, the most prominent feature
being the spire which dominates
the surroundings. Four stained-
glass windows by Robert Paterson
1941, Douglas Hamilton 1954 and
Linda Fraser 1986. Embroidered pew
and chair cushions and seasonal
banners designed by Pat Hodgson of
Hawksland, Lesmahagow and worked
by members of the congregation.

* Sunday: 11.00am and 6.30pm
* Open by arrangement (01555 895593)

131 ST NICHOLAS PARISH CHURCH, LANARK

**The Cross
Lanark
ML11 9DZ**

A NS 881 437

Church of Scotland

www.lanarkstnicholas.co.uk

By John Reid of Nemphlar 1774. Large two-storey classical box with a square tower and steeple, standing prominently at the bottom of the High Street. There is a 2.4m (8ft) statue of William Wallace in the steeple, sculpted by Robert Forrest. Stained glass, baptismal font in Caen stone. Fine pipe organ. Church exterior restored 2008–9.

- Sunday: 11.00am; Wednesday: 10.15am
- Open 10.00am–12.00 noon, 1st Wednesday of the month, or by arrangement (01555 666220)

132 GREYFRIARS PARISH CHURCH, LANARK

**Bloomgate
Lanark
ML11 9ET**

A NS 880 437

Church of Scotland

www.webartz.com/greyfriars

William Leiper designed this, his smallest church, in 1875 for the Bloomgate United Presbyterian Congregation. Its simple Gothic interior is enlivened by a slender bellcote inspired by Andrew Heiton's Findlater Church in Dublin. Two-manual pipe organ by Ingram, recently fully refurbished. Pulpit fall and welcome banner by local artist Myra Gibson.

- Sunday: 11.00am
- Open by arrangement (01555 663363)

SOUTH LANARKSHIRE

 133 CHRIST CHURCH, LANARK

**Hope Street
Lanark
ML11 7NE**

NS 881 439

Scottish Episcopal

www.christchurchlanark.com

Gothic church of a simple rectangle with aisles of 1853 by John Henderson. Carving by Major General Stevenson. Modern stained-glass window with Celtic saints by Pauline Payne, art teacher of Lanark Grammar School in the 1960s and 1970s.

- 10.30am each Sunday, 8.30am 1st Sunday and 6.00pm 2nd Sunday of the month
- Open by arrangement (01555 663065)

   (in halls)

134 ST MARY'S, LANARK

**70 Bannatyne Street
Lanark
ML11 7JS**

NS 886 435

Roman Catholic

www.stmaryslanark.org.uk

Gothic Revival cruciform church by Dublin architects Ashlin & Coleman 1908. Graceful 44m (144ft) spire. Remarkable interior decoration including imposing reredos of Caen stone and marble, statues of St Mungo, St Margaret and St Columba and fine stained glass.

- Saturday: Vigil 6.30pm; Sunday: 9.30am, 11.00am and 6.30pm; weekdays: 9.30am
- Open during daylight hours (01555 662234)

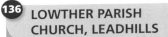

135 ST MARY'S, LARKHALL

**Raploch Road
Larkhall
ML9 1AN**

⚔ NS 757 509

⛪ Roman Catholic

Linked with St Bride's, East Kilbride
(120)

Founded as a mission in 1861, the
present church was built 1872.
Rectangular freestyle church with
overhanging eaves and harled walls
with painted surrounds to doors
and windows. Inside, pointed arches
divide the nave from the aisles.

- Saturday: Mass 6.30pm; Sunday:
  8.00am, 10.45am, 4.30pm (winter),
  6.00pm (summer)
- Open by arrangement (01698 882564)

   (in halls)

136 LOWTHER PARISH CHURCH, LEADHILLS

**Leadhills
ML12 6XP**

⚔ NS 885 148

⛪ Church of Scotland

On B797 near south end of village

The lead-mining village of Leadhills
is the highest village in Scotland. The
church, designed by John B. Wilson,
was built in 1883 as the United Free
Church; it amalgamated with the
parish church in 1937. Two-manual
pedal organ and an electronic organ.
Memorial window depicting *Dorcas*.

- Sunday: 11.30am
- Open 1st Sunday of the month or by
  arrangement (01659 74326)

SOUTH LANARKSHIRE

137 LESMAHAGOW OLD PARISH CHURCH

**Church Square
Abbeygreen
Lesmahagow
ML11 0EJ**

Å NS 814 399

🏠 Church of Scotland

🌐 www.lopc.org.uk

King David I granted a church and lands to the Tironensian monks in 1144. He also granted the right of sanctuary, violated in 1335 when the church was burned, with villagers inside, by John Eltham, brother of Edward I of England. The present church was built in 1803 and the apse added in the 1890s. Pipe organ 1889. Several stained-glass windows, including one whose central panel, *The Descent from the Cross*, is a copy of the painting by Rubens in Antwerp Cathedral. The bell is dated 1625. Display in the chapterhouse.

- Sunday: 10.00am
- Open by arrangement (01555 892425)

138 LIBBERTON AND QUOTHQUAN PARISH CHURCH

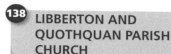

**Libberton
ML11 8LX**

Å NS 992 428

🏠 Church of Scotland

Linked with Biggar Kirk (103), Black Mount Parish Church (117), Culter Parish Church (115)

On B7016 from Biggar to Carnwath

Carnwath was separated from Libberton in 1186, and Quothquan parish was joined to Libberton in 1660. Quothquan Church (about 3km (2 miles) from Libberton) is now a ruin; its aisle is the burial place of the Chancellor family. The new church was built on an ancient site of worship at Libberton in 1812 and restored in 1902. It has fine woodwork and memorials of distinction.

- Sunday: 9.30am, 10.45am and 12.00 noon on a quarterly rotation with Black Mount and Culter
- Open by arrangement (01899 220625)

139 PETTINAIN CHURCH

**Pettinain
ML11 8SS**

NS 955 429

Former Church of Scotland

www.srct.org.uk

11km (7 miles) east of Lanark, between A73 and A70

Fine example of a rural parish kirk, with outstanding views across open countryside. The site has been a place of worship since the early 12th century when David I established the Chapel of 'Pedynane'. The present church dates principally from the 18th century with an earlier belfry of 1692 and an incised cross slab reused as a relieving lintel. Interesting walled burial ground. Acquired by the Scottish Redundant Churches Trust in 2000 with the generous support of local people.

- Occasional; weddings and funerals by arrangement
- Open by arrangement (01334 472032)

140 DOUGLAS WATER AND RIGSIDE CHURCH, RIGSIDE

**Ayr Road
Rigside
ML11 9NP**

NS 873 347

Church of Scotland

www.douglasvalleychurch.org

Linked with St Bride's, Douglas (118)

Follow signs to golf course

The church was built in 1885–6 as Douglas Water Free Church on land gifted by Lord Home. The sanctuary was refurbished in 1939. The building originally had a small belfry, now demolished, and the bell now hangs on a frame beside the church.

- Sunday: 11.30am September to June, other arrangements July and August
- Open by arrangement (01555 850000)

WC

141 RUTHERGLEN OLD PARISH CHURCH

**Main Street
Rutherglen
G73 1JP**

NS 613 617

Church of Scotland

www.rutherglen.clara.co.uk/
index.htm

Junction with Queen Street

The present church was designed by the architect J. J. Burnet 1902 in Gothic style, the fourth on this site since the original foundation in the 6th century. The gable end of an 11th-century church still stands in the graveyard supporting St Mary's steeple (15th century). It contains the church bell 1635. Stained glass, including a First World War Memorial. Communion cups dated 1665 are still in use. The churchyard occupies an ancient site, at its gateway two stone offertory shelters, and a sundial set above its entrance dated 1679.

- Sunday: 11.00am
- Open 2nd Saturday of each month, 10.00am–12.00 noon (0141 647 6178)

142 ST COLUMBKILLE'S CHURCH, RUTHERGLEN

**Main Street
Rutherglen
G73 2SL**

NS 614 616

Roman Catholic

www.stcolumbkilles.co.uk

Magnificent church, Coia 1940, replacing original church founded in 1851. Modern adaptation of an Italian basilica in red brick with stone margins. Massive façade with five tall windows and five statues by Archibald Dawson of Christ and the four Evangelists. Sacred Heart Chapel by Walter Pritchard. Stations of the Cross by Miss McGeechan.

- Saturday: Vigil Mass 5.30pm; Sunday: Masses 9.00am, 10.30am, 12.00 noon and 7.00pm
- Open Monday to Thursday 9.00am–5.00pm, Friday 9.00am–2.00pm (0141 647 6034)

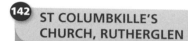

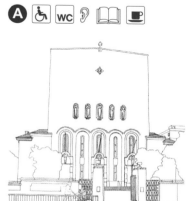

143 PATERSON CHURCH, STONEHOUSE

**Lawrie Street
Stonehouse
ML9 3LN**

⚔ NS 755 469

⛪ United Free Church

The current building, named after Rev. Henry Angus Paterson who ministered to the congregation for over 60 years, dates from 1879. Designed by Shiells & Thomson, it is a Gothic-style church with a square corner tower and a rose window above the door. Remained a United Free Church at the Union of 1929. Refurbished following a fire in 1977. Fine collection of stained-glass windows by Crear McCartney.

- Sunday: 10.00am
- Open Tuesday mid-June to end of August 10.00am–12.00 noon (01698 793876)

144 AVENDALE OLD PARISH CHURCH, STRATHAVEN

**59a Kirk Street
Strathaven
ML10 6LB**

⚔ NS 701 443

⛪ Church of Scotland

🌐 www.avendale-drumclog.com

Linked with Drumclog Memorial Kirk (119)

Records show a church in Strathaven in 1288. This church was built 1772 and the interior renovated 1879. The centre section of the south gallery was reserved for the family and tenants of the Duke of Hamilton and is known as 'The Duke's Gallery'. Stained-glass window of the Last Supper, Crear McCartney 1996.

- Sunday: 11.00am. Details of evening services on church website
- Open Monday to Friday 9.00am–12.00 noon (not school holidays), or by arrangement (01357 521939)

SOUTH LANARKSHIRE

145 EAST PARISH CHURCH, STRATHAVEN

**Green Street
Strathaven
ML10 6LT**

NS 702 446

Church of Scotland

Linked with Glasford Parish Church (121)

The building, with its tall tower and spire, is a local landmark. Built in 1777 as a tall hall-church with clock tower added 1843. Major rebuilding 1877. Prominent pulpit and memorial windows.

- Sunday: 11.30am
- Open by arrangement (01357 521138)

B ♿ WC ☞

146 STRATHAVEN WEST CHURCH

**Townhead Street
Strathaven
ML10 6DJ**

NS 700 444

Church of Scotland

Originally a Relief Church out of Strathaven East, dedicated 1835, it was conceived with enthusiasm, built and dedicated within nine months. Design based on Carluke Church. Pipe organ 1930. Two major refurbishments, for centenary and sesquicentenary, resulting in a surprisingly warm, attractive interior. War Memorial in vestibule. Two memorial stained-glass windows.

- Sunday: 11.00am
- Open by arrangement (01357 529086)

B ♿ WC ☞

147 ST PATRICK'S CHURCH, STRATHAVEN

52 Stonehouse Road
Strathaven
ML10 6LF

NS 706 445

Roman Catholic

www.stpatricks-strathaven.com

Built 1901, to serve the growing Catholic population of Strathaven following immigration from Ireland and the Highlands, and paid for by Archbishop Charles Eyre of Glasgow. Sanctuary extension and porch added 1953. The original smaller church, built 1853, stands besides the church and is now a parish hall.

- Saturday: 10.00am, Vigil 6.00pm; Sunday: 9.00am and 11.00am; weekdays: 9.30am
- Open by arrangement (01357 520104)

148 SYMINGTON KIRK

Kirk Bauk
Symington
ML12 6LB

NS 999 352

Church of Scotland

www.symingtonkirk.com

Linked with Cairngryffe Kirk, Kirkmichael (112)

The original church was established c. 1160. The present building is largely from the 18th and 19th centuries, and the belfry is 1734. Watchtower in graveyard. A feature of the interior is the scissorbeam roof.

- Sunday: 9.30am or 11.00am as indicated on notice-board
- Open by arrangement (01899 308838)

 (in halls)

SOUTH LANARKSHIRE

SOUTH LANARKSHIRE

149 TARBRAX CHURCH

**Tarbrax Road
Tarbrax
EH55 8XA**

⚐ NT 025 549
⛪ Church of Scotland

Linked with Auchengray Church (102)

1.5km (1 mile) west of A70

Attractively simple church built in 1919 to serve the mining community of that time. Designed by Peter MacGregor Chalmers. The mine has long since gone, but the church continues with a surprisingly cosmopolitan congregation.

- Sunday: September to June, 10.30am; no services July and August
- Open by arrangement (01501 785234)

150 ST ANDREW'S, UDDINGSTON

**4 Bothwell Road
Uddingston
G71 7ET**

⚐ NS 697 601
⛪ Scottish Episcopal

Linked with St Cuthbert's, Cambuslang (108)

Built 1890, architect Miles Septimus Gibson; foundation stone laid by Lady Mary Alice Douglas-Home, aunt of the later Prime Minister, Sir Alec Douglas-Home. After a fire in 1993, the chancel was restored by Alex Braidwood of Blantyre. Stained glass by J. T. & C. E. Stewart of Glasgow and Peter Berry of Malmesbury. The Blackett & Howden pipe organ, damaged in the fire, awaits restoration. Painting of Bothwell Castle by architect and local historian J. Jeffrey Waddell.

- Sunday: 11.15am
- Open by arrangement (01698 812536)

151 ARTHURLIE PARISH CHURCH, BARRHEAD

**Ralston Road
Barrhead
G78 2QQ**

NS 501 588

Church of Scotland

www.arthurliechurch.org.uk

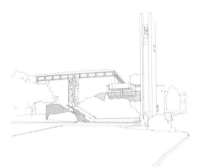

Junction with Main Street

Built 1967 to replace the 1796 'whitewashed kirk'. Designed by Honeyman, Jack & Robertson of Glasgow. High roof and long aisles. The open pews, constructed from the same light hardwood (ramin) as the cross, font, lectern and choir stalls, create an understated unity. Stained glass by Gordon Webster in the style 'Dalles de Verre'. The grounds, laid out by Bessie McWhirter, are open to all.

- Sunday: 9.30am and 11.00am; Wednesday: 10.45am
- Open by arrangement (0141 881 1792)

152 ST JOHN'S, BARRHEAD

**Aurs Road
Barrhead
G78 2RW**

NS 508 592

Roman Catholic

www.stjohns-barrhead.co.uk

Built in 1961, architect Thomas S. Cordiner, after the old building was burnt down in 1941, before its centenary Mass. Note the prevalence of Greek iconography over Latin and the recurrence of the motif of St John. Tabernacle door designed by Hew Lorimer and presidential chair by John McLachlan. Rushworth & Dreaper organ.

- Saturday: Vigil 4.30pm; Sunday: 10.00am, 12.00 noon and 6.30pm; weekdays: 10.00am
- Open by arrangement (0141 876 1553)

153 GREENBANK CHURCH, CLARKSTON

**36 Eaglesham Road
Clarkston
G76 7DJ**

NS 574 568

Church of Scotland

www.greenbankglasgow.org.uk

The church, designed by McKissack & Rowan, was opened in 1884. The chancel, furnishings and stained-glass windows (James Ballantine) were added in 1937. A mural by Alasdair Gray in the transept was completed in 1979. The centenary chapel was opened in 1984.

- Sunday: 10.30am. See website for other services
- Open by arrangement (0141 644 1841)

154 ST AIDAN'S, CLARKSTON

**Mearns Road
Clarkston
G76 7LZ**

NS 573 574

Scottish Episcopal

www.staidans.freeserve.co.uk

Hall-church built 1924 and present church 1951, architects Noad & Wallace. The building has a steel frame and brick interior. Red sandstone facing matches hall. Stained glass includes a pair of windows by Susan Bradbury 1998.

- Sunday: Holy Communion 8.00am, Sung Eucharist 10.00am, Evensong/ Evening Prayer 6.30pm
- Open Wednesday 9.00–11.30am (0141 577 0196)

155 ## STAMPERLAND CHURCH, CLARKSTON

Stamperland Gardens
Clarkston
G76 8LJ

NS 576 581

Church of Scotland

http://myweb.tiscali.co.uk/
stamperland/index.htm

The congregation's first service was held in an air-raid shelter of a local garage in 1940. Thereafter, a local shop was occupied until a church was built in 1941 (now the hall). The present modern building was erected in 1964, architect J. Thompson King & Partners. Concrete bell-tower. Three stained-glass windows by Gordon Webster, previously in Woodside Parish Church. Pipe organ 1897 by Lewis & Co. from Regent Place United Presbyterian Church, Dennistoun, Glasgow. Furnishings include items from 1938 Glasgow Empire Exhibition Church. Bas-relief of mythical pelican on outside wall.

- Sunday: 11.00am
- Open by arrangement (0141 638 3502)

 156 ## ST JOSEPH'S, CLARKSTON

2 Eaglesham Road
Clarkston
G76 7BT

NS 575 572

Roman Catholic

www.stjosephsclarkston.org

First church built also as a school in 1880. Replaced by a modern building on same site in 1971. Stained-glass windows by Shona McInnes and tapestries by Joanna Kinnersly-Taylor.

- Saturday: 10.00am, Vigil 6.00pm; Sunday: 8.30am, 10.00am, 12.00 noon and 6.00pm; weekdays: 10.00am and 7.00pm
- Open daily (0141 644 2640)

157 EAGLESHAM PARISH CHURCH

**Montgomery Street
Eaglesham
G76 0AS**

Ⓐ NS 574 519

🏠 Church of Scotland

🌐 www.eagleshamparishchurch.
co.uk

The present attractive church with clock steeple was designed by Robert McLachlane and completed in 1790. It replaced churches on this site since early times. Former United Free Church is now the church halls, and Carswell United Presbyterian Church refurbished as the Carswell Halls (both located on Montgomery Street). 'Father' Willis organ and fine embroidered pulpit falls by Kathleen Whyte and Fiona Hamilton. Covenanter graves in churchyard.

- Sunday: 11.00am
- Open Tuesday and Thursday, June to September, 2.00–4.00pm or by arrangement (01355 302087)

158 ST BRIDGET'S, EAGLESHAM

**12 Polnoon Street
Eaglesham
G76 0BH**

Ⓐ NS 572 521

🏠 Roman Catholic

Built 1858 to provide a local place of worship for Catholic villagers, many of whom had settled as refugees from the Irish potato famine. Land provided by 13th Earl of Eglinton behind 'Mayfield', a house in Polnoon Street, now Chapel House. Interior enhanced by Californian redwood beams and a large canvas of the *Deposition of Christ from the Cross* by de Surne. Statue of Madonna and Child from Ireland. Interior refurbished in 1960s.

- Sunday: 11.00am
- Open by arrangement (01355 303298)

159 ORCHARDHILL PARISH CHURCH

**12 Church Road
Giffnock
G46 6JR**

NS 563 587

Church of Scotland

www.orchardhill.org.uk

East side of Fenwick Road, north of Eastwood Toll

Church and hall built in Gothic Revival style, H. E. Clifford 1900. Of local stone with a red tiled roof, squat tower with spiral wooden stair and roof turret. Extensions carried out in 1910 and 1935. Stained glass 1936–86 by Webster, McLellan, Wilson and Clark. Wood panelling 1900–35. Two-manual pipe organ, Hill, Norman & Beard. Embroidered pulpit falls 1993.

- Sunday: 9.45am, 11.15am and 6.30pm (part-year only)
- Open by arrangement (0141 571 7153)

160 GIFFNOCK SOUTH PARISH CHURCH

**2 Greenhill Avenue
Giffnock
G46 6QX**

NS 559 582

Church of Scotland

www.giffnocksouth.co.uk

A hall-church (now Eglinton Hall) was opened in 1914. The present church was begun in 1921 and dedicated in 1929. It is by Stewart & Paterson in late Gothic style built of blonde sandstone. There is a fine collection of stained-glass windows, including six by Gordon Webster. There are three recent windows, one by Sadie McLellan and two by Brian Hutchison.

- Sunday: 11.00am
- Open by arrangement (0141 638 2599)

161 NETHERLEE PARISH CHURCH

**130 Ormonde Avenue
Netherlee
Glasgow
G44 3RT**

NS 577 590

Church of Scotland

www.netherleechurch.org

Junction of Ormonde Avenue and Ormonde Drive

Built in neo-Gothic style of red Dumfriesshire sandstone by Stewart & Paterson 1934. Oak panelling and furnishings beautifully carved. Lovely stained glass by Herbert Hendrie (including chancel window of 1935), Gordon Webster, William Wilson and Sadie McLellan.

- September to May, 11.00am and some at 6.30pm, and 10.00am Wednesday; June to August, 10.00am and 11.00am
- Open by arrangement (0141 637 2503)

162 NEILSTON PARISH CHURCH

**Main Street
Neilston
G78 3ET**

NS 480 574

Church of Scotland

www.neilstonparishchurch.org.uk

There has been a Christian presence on the site for over 1,000 years. Originally a single-storey building, the church was enlarged 1746–98, including the balcony. Further alterations 1820. An important feature is a Gothic window above the vault of the Mure family of Caldwell. Stained glass by Stephen Adam. Nearby is a memorial to John Robertson, a native of Neilston, who built the engine for the *Comet*, the first steamship on the Clyde. Circular mort-house of 1817.

- Sunday: 11.00am
- Open by arrangement (0141 881 9445)

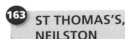 **ST THOMAS'S, NEILSTON**

**70 Main Street
Neilston
G78 3NJ**

NS 479 573

Roman Catholic

St Thomas's chapel and school were built in 1861 following an influx of Irish workers escaping the potato famine in Ireland. Dedicated to St Thomas the Apostle as a tribute to the work to make the parish succeed. The tower was added in 1891.

- Saturday: Vigil 6.00pm; Sunday: 9.00am, 10.00am; Monday to Saturday: 10.00am
- Open daily (0141 881 1478)

 BROOM PARISH CHURCH, NEWTON MEARNS

**Mearns Road
Newton Mearns
G77 5HN**

NS 554 563

Church of Scotland

www.broomchurch.org.uk

Junction of Mearns Road and Broom Road East

A dual-purpose hall/church, now the Ninian Hall, was erected in 1941, and the present church, designed by Honeyman, Jack & Robertson, was opened in 1959. The adjacent Columba Hall was added in 1967. The church interior is enlivened by the modern version of a cruck frame with trusses rising from floor to ceiling. Both the stained-glass windows in the church were designed by Ralph Cowan.

- Sunday: 10.00am
- Open by arrangement (0141 639 3528)

165 **MEARNS PARISH CHURCH, NEWTON MEARNS**

Mearns Road
Newton Mearns
G77 5LZ

⚐ NS 543 551

🏠 Church of Scotland

🌐 www.mearnsparishkirk.co.uk

Junction with Eaglesham Road

Religious settlement and site since AD 800, the present church dates from 1813 and was extensively renovated in 1932. Organ originally from Glasgow City Hall. Stained-glass windows by Gordon Webster and James McPhie. South-wall tapestry donated by the late Lord Goold. A phosphor-bronze weathercock weighing 2.5 cwt atop the bell-tower was erected in the late 1940s. Gateposts in the form of sentry boxes date from the era of the Resurrectionists.

- Sunday: 9.30am and 11.00am September to June, 10.30am July and August
- Open by arrangement (0141 639 7373)

 (by arrangement)

166 **MAXWELL MEARNS CASTLE CHURCH**

Waterfoot Road
Newton Mearns
G77 5RE

⚐ NS 553 553

🏠 Church of Scotland

🌐 www.maxwellmearns.org.uk

Dramatically situated on a hilltop and attached to an A-listed 15th-century castle keep (now in need of renovation) is this 1970s modern circular sanctuary, by Walter Ramsay Architects. The large suite of halls houses facilities for congregational life. Stained glass transferred from the original Maxwell Parish Church in Pollok Street, Tradeston and from Govanhill Parish Church. Concrete cross sculpture within the sanctuary and a wonderful collection of banners.

- Sunday: 10.30am and 7.30pm
- Open by arrangement (0141 639 5169)

  (in halls)

167 CALDWELL PARISH CHURCH

**Neilston Road
Uplawmoor
G78 4AB**

NS 435 552

Church of Scotland

Linked with Dunlop Parish Church, Ayrshire (*Sacred South-West Scotland* (54))

Off B736 Barrhead-to-Irvine Road

Simple country church built 1889 by William Ingram. Memorial glass sculpture depicting the Trinity by Ralph Cowan 1989. Garden of Remembrance dedicated 1997.

- Sunday: 10.00am
- Open by arrangement (01505 850315)

168 WILLIAMWOOD PARISH CHURCH

**4 Vardar Avenue
Clarkston
G76 7QP**

NS 567 576

Church of Scotland

 www.williamwoodparishchurch.org.uk

Junction with Seres Road, Clarkston

Built in 1937 as a Church Extension charge in red brick with a short bell-tower, the church is a fine example of mid-1930s church architecture and was designed by James M. Honeyman. The original and somewhat austere interior has been upgraded and enriched. Historical and other information available.

- Sunday: 11.00am
- Open February to June and September to December, weekdays, 9.45am–12.00 noon (0141 638 2091)

Index

References are to each church's entry number in the gazetteer.

SACRED GLASGOW AND THE CLYDE VALLEY